UR

You Are Who You Choose To Be

ROB COOK

UR: You Are Who You Choose To Be

Copyright © 2017 Rob Cook, Claremont, California

All rights reserved.

ISBN-13: 978-1532876363

ISBN-10: 153287636X

Library of Congress Control Number: 2017900600

Edited by John Bilwin and Sean Porritt

Graphic images used from pixabay.com

Cover photo taken by Rob Cook

This book can be found on Amazon or purchased at:
https://www.createspace.com/6224973

The Facebook page for UR is:
https://www.facebook.com/URRobCook

I want to give a special thanks to my family and friends, those that have supported me in all that I have done, my children who are my love and legacy and my wife Jacqueline who is the love of my life.

CONTENTS

Chapter	Title	Page
	Preface	viii
1	Aging	1
2	Appropriateness & Politeness	2
3	Attitude	3
4	Be Positive	4
5	Behavior	5
6	Behavior Altering Substances	6
7	Being Happy vs. Sad	7
8	Boundaries & Improvement	8
9	Career & Success	9
10	Caring	11
11	Children	12
12	Cleanliness & Appearance	13
13	Charity	14
14	Choices	15
15	Commitment	16
16	Common Sense	17
17	Communication	18
18	Communication (Non-Verbal)	20
19	Control & Responsibility	21
20	Creativity	22
21	Decisions	23
22	Demeanor	24
23	Difficulty	25

24	Dream	26
25	Education & Intellectual Curiosity	27
26	Enjoyment, Fun, Laughter	29
27	Entitlement	30
28	Environment	31
29	Ethnicity, Race & Family Heritage	32
30	Examples	33
31	Expectations	34
32	Expectation Setting	36
33	Experience	37
34	Exploration & Innovation	38
35	Failure	39
36	Family	40
37	Fighting & Self-Defense	42
38	Focus	43
39	Forgiveness	44
40	Freedom	45
41	Friendship	47
42	Goals	48
43	GOD	49
44	Government & Politics	50
45	Gratitude	51
46	Greed & Power	52
47	Hard Work, Motor, Drive	53
48	Health, Nutrition, Fitness	55
49	Hospitals & Medicine	56

50	Humility	58
51	IDK	59
52	Integrity, Honor, Ethics	61
53	Know Yourself, Then Improve Yourself	62
54	Laws & Authority	63
55	Leadership & Inspiration	64
56	Living & Dying	65
57	Love	66
58	Loyalty	68
59	Make the Best of Situations	69
60	Marriage	70
61	Media	72
62	Messages & Intent	73
63	Money	74
64	Music, Art, Science	76
65	Nature vs. Nurture	77
66	Negotiation, Risk & Reward	78
67	Observant & Detailed	79
68	Opportunities	80
69	Others First	82
70	Parents	83
71	Past, Present, Future	85
72	Patience & Waiting	86
73	Patriotism	87
74	Perfection	88
75	Perseverance & Persistence	89

76	Perspective	90
77	Preparation	92
78	Pride	93
79	Priorities	94
80	Problem Solving	97
81	Quotes	98
82	Relationships	100
83	Rest, Sleep, Vacation	101
84	Secret to Life	102
85	Second Wind (Not Quitting)	103
86	Self-Confidence	104
87	Self-Satisfaction	105
88	Sex & Sexuality	106
89	Siblings	107
90	Social Issues	108
91	Spouse	110
92	Strong of Mind & Courageous	111
93	Taxes	112
94	Teach Your Children	113
95	Time Management	114
96	Things Out of Your Control	115
97	Things You Truly Own	116
98	Thinking - Reading, Writing, Talking & Listening	117
99	Timing	119
100	Tragedy	120
101	Trust	121

102	Unlearn Bad Thoughts & Habits	122
103	Values	123
104	Wanting, Wishing, Regret	125
105	Worry	126
	Final Thoughts	127
	About the Author	128

PREFACE

The purpose of this text is to write down my view of the world and how I see my place in it. Most of the writing was done on my smartphone in my spare time. I believe my views are not much different from most other men my age and I did not write this in an effort to be politically correct or promote any particular political view. My views have been acquired through the relationships and interactions I have had with family and numerous friends over the years. I have been fortunate over my lifetime to have had many great friendships with many ethical, caring people of high integrity. You know who you are. Particularly, my wife Jacqueline, my best friend and love of my life and my children Chelsea and Grant who are now adults. Chelsea, who has always been my Cosette, is married to Sean (in whom I have great faith) and they have my first grandson Giacomo and granddaughter Alessia on the way. Grant who's strong character and work ethic will make him a far better man than me. My Uncle Ron and Aunt Dana, my father's sister, and my Uncle Ed, my mother's brother, and Aunt Mary have all been wonderful examples which I have cherished my whole life.

Most of all, I am writing this in remembrance of my parents, for all that I have learned and become because of their love and support. My father, Robert "Bob" Frank Cook, passed away on April 20, 2014 in what was a short battle with lung and brain cancer. Just after he died, I found myself on his sofa at 6 A.M. thinking about the wonderful example he and my mother, Alice Anna Bilwin Cook, were for me and how lucky I was to have spent so much time with them. I thought about the values they had instilled in me, with their words, but more so through their actions and how they lived their lives.

My father was born in El Paso, Texas in 1939 to Dan and Geraldine Cook with his sister Dana. Dan was the Constable in El Paso and in the early 1940's they moved to Los Angeles and then Baldwin Park, where he worked for the railroads while in California. His wife Geraldine was a nurse and avid amateur geologist. Bob graduated from Baldwin Park High School in 1957, and then attended Mount San Antonio Junior College. He served in the Navy on the USS Yorktown until 1962. In 1968 he married my mother Alice Bilwin in Boston, Massachusetts. He owned a Mobil gas station in the City of

Industry, until the early 1970's and then got his private pilot license. He owned several planes, got his commercial license and taught others to fly at Brackett Field in La Verne and Chino Airport in California. In the early 1980's, he flew commercially for Air Cortez, often to Baja California and Las Vegas. In 1984, he went to work as an auto mechanic teacher for Hacienda La Puente School where he spent 20 years. He also worked for Rio Hondo Community College and Cerritos College in the automotive program. He was very mechanically inclined and he enjoyed tinkering, building and rebuilding everything. No one was more helpful to others and giving of his time and expertise than my father.

My mother was born in Dorchester, Massachusetts November 1937 to John and Anna Bilwin, originally from Russia and Poland with her brother Ed. John was a blacksmith. Although they did not speak much English they insisted my mother only speak English. She loved art and went to school at what is now Northeastern University in Boston. She became a grade school teacher and moved to San Diego in the early 1960's in her VW bug. She married my father in 1968 in Boston and they settled in West Covina California, where they lived most of their adult lives. I was born in 1969, their only son. Following my birth my mother had various health issues including being in a coma and paralysis on her left side. I was cared for by my grandparents who lived fairly close. Although my mother recovered from these setbacks in the mid 1970's, she was diagnosed with kidney disease and in 1980 had a kidney transplant. The transplant had a 40% chance of working. The transplant worked for about 5 years, which at the time was considered successful. The toughest part was the regiment of medications she took to prevent the body from rejecting the kidney. Steroids are difficult on the body. She remained on dialysis for the next 30 plus years, which is longer than most people survive. Her strength to persevere was matched only by her constant effort to not act or let others know she was sick. She had a great attitude about life and was always positive. She also had the constant undying support, commitment and love for and from my father. A lesser man would not have lasted through the sickness, money issues and time in hospitals. My mother's true passion was art. She was constantly creating something. From ceramics to ink drawings, oil canvas to acrylic & watercolor paintings. A collection of her work can be seen at https://www.pinterest.com/BilwinCook/.

I don't pretend to be a psychologist, I have just written what I believe and what works for me. My hope is that in the future this text may provide comfort and insight for my future family about how I lived and what I believe, not necessarily as a guide, but one way, my way, to look at the world. It seems to me that history repeats itself and I hope that sharing my view can be helpful to others. I don't always follow my own advice, but I do the best I can.

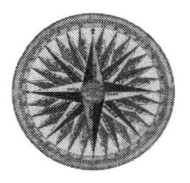

"I find the great thing in this world is not so much where we stand, as in what direction we are moving: To reach the port of heaven, we must sail sometimes with the wind and sometimes against it, -- but we must sail, and not drift, nor lie at anchor."
-- Oliver Wendell Holmes

1 AGING

Stay active in body and mind. A body in motion stays in motion, basic physics. A body at rest remains at rest. Get out of the house; challenge your body and mind. Getting older can prove to be mentally and physically challenging. Prepare your mind and body now for the challenge. This is the battle we all hope to face and that we know is coming.

Always have goals and things to do. Plan vacations, daily activities, etc.

Take care of your body, stay off ladders, but do as much as you can. Father Time may not be defeated, however, stay positive and productive.

Surround yourself with active people. Smile and remain young at heart. Embrace the concept of mind over matter.

UR *as old as you feel!*

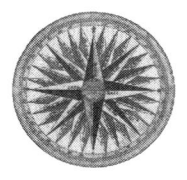

"Dost thou love life? Then do not squander time, for that's the stuff life is made of."
-- Benjamin Franklin (1706-1790)

2 APPROPRIATENESS & POLITENESS

In basketball they discuss situational awareness. Players should know the score, number of fouls they have and time left on the clock. This way you can make appropriate decisions based on the situation. In the same way, your behavior in life should fit the situation based on the people, environment and your values. It may sound simple, but it is important. Be solemn at funerals, be happy at parties and be true to yourself and who you are. Know when to do the talking and when to do the listening.

Be polite whenever possible. How you behave represents you, your family, your faith, your school, your community and your country.

Understand that others are entitled to their opinions, but you are entitled to yours. You can respectively disagree with others and still have your own opinion. Be a respectful lady or gentleman and you will likely become a respected lady or gentleman.

"Nothing is ever lost by courtesy. It is the cheapest of pleasures, costs nothing, and conveys much."
-- Erastus Wiman

3 ATTITUDE

Attitude determines altitude! Be in control of how you behave and what you do and say. It's no fun to be around someone with a bad attitude, especially when it's YOU!

You can't control others behavior or attitude, so don't try. Be the example, focus on your attitude. Be constructive and positive; seek solutions rather than focusing only on problems or potential issues. Have a good outlook on yourself, your life, your friends and family, your work and the world. You get to control your attitude. Don't use excuses.

What are you like when you wake up in the morning, when you get tired, when you get hungry, or when you meet someone for the first time? Your attitude creates the environment around you, for yourself and others; make it great!

Head up, shoulders back. Don't feel sorry for yourself, it's a waste of time. Be proud of yourself and who you choose to be.

UR *the attitude you display!*

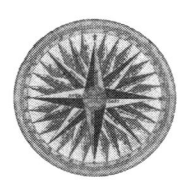

"The greatest discovery of my generation is that man can alter his life simply by altering his attitude of mind."
-- William James

4 BE POSITIVE

Train yourself to think positively! Be positive about everything as often as possible, but genuine in your beliefs. Believe in the possible! It isn't fun to be around someone who is constantly negative, but it is important to be balanced in your thinking.

In college, one of my professors performed a class experiment. He asked us to write down all the things we could use a wheel barrel for; the class came up with about 30 uses. As we got close to 30 the class really struggled to come up with ideas. However, when we were asked to come up with the things we couldn't use a wheel barrel for the ideas were free flowing. The class came up with over 100 ideas and there would have been more if we didn't stop. The point is to manage your thoughts to be constructive and positive as often as possible. Your thoughts and ideas should be limitless. Try to find solutions instead of problems, ways for others to be successful instead of fail, and provide answers instead of questions. Also, surround yourself with others who are positive and treat you with respect and you will have a better, happier, more self-satisfying life.

UR *as positive as you choose to be.*

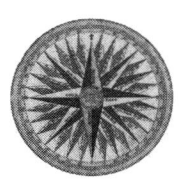

"When one door of happiness closes, another opens; but often we look so long at the closed door that we do not see the one which has been opened for us."
-- Helen Keller

5 BEHAVIOR

How do you act? What things do you do and what does it say about who you are and what you believe?

Behavior is the outward expression of your attitude. What you do or don't do is a real reflection of who you are.

Make your behaviors positive and reflective of your true belief to be a trustworthy person. Leaders behave consistently so that others understand their values and beliefs. Phil Jackson, former coach of the Bulls and Lakers, provides us with a great example of how to use behavior to set expectations for his teams. When his teams weren't playing well he would not call a time out or yell and scream. He was calm and very purposeful about what he said. That sent the message to his teams that, 1.) It's up to them to figure out how to play better, 2.) They needed to own their own performance as the player on the court, and 3.) Don't panic, solve the problem. I think he indirectly sent all these messages as he sat quietly on the bench during the game and in the manner in which he addressed the players and the game.

Timing and situational awareness is also critical when thinking about behavior. Try to view your own behaviors through the eyes of others, peers, elders, and youth to get a real perspective on what is appropriate or not and to have a real sense of who you really are.

Ultimately, be true to yourself and who you are and then behave accordingly.

UR *the behaviors you display.*

"The nearest way to glory -- a shortcut, as it were -- is to strive to be what you wish to be thought to be."
-- Socrates, quoted in Cicero, 44 BC.

6 BEHAVIOR ALTERING SUBSTANCES

Think carefully before taking anything that alters your behavior or view of reality. Don't allow substances (or others) to control you. Own your life and the outcomes of all your decisions. Be courageous. Be proud of your actions, even the mistakes if you did your best. Sometimes you can't control the outcomes, just your effort.

Consider the "newspaper" or "grandmother" test before you make a dumb decision. That is.... would you be comfortable having a front-page article in the newspaper about your decision or would you be comfortable telling your grandmother what you have done? Generally, if you're ok with these two tests it couldn't be too bad.

I don't think using drugs and alcohol make you a bad person. I do believe it leads to bad decisions and bad behaviors. I also think it demonstrates a lack of pride, self-confidence, self-control and weak-mindedness. If you find yourself dependent or addicted to a substance, be strong enough to ask for help.

Do not associate with people that condone the use of drugs and alcohol to alter reality. Not just because of the substances, but that their way of thinking about themselves, others and the world must not be right, if they think what they are doing is right.

Remember you are who you associate with.

I personally have a very low tolerance for this and don't understand why this is so difficult for so many to control themselves. Focus on the loves in your life, family and the wonders of this world. There is plenty to keep your mind engaged and energized. Keep your priorities straight.

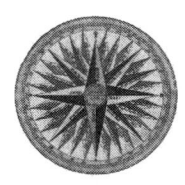

"Ignorance is curable, stupid is terminal."
-A fellow Juror

7 BEING HAPPY VS. SAD

I truly believe there is an appropriate time and place for everything. We are emotional beings and there is a place in our lives for being happy and for being sad. I am reminded of the phrase, if you never had a bad day, you'd never know what a good one looks like. Life is relative to your past experiences. This is why the more mature you are, the better perspective you should have.

Sadness is an appropriate state of being when something you have worked hard for or someone you love is gone. However, keep your perspective, elongated times of sadness lead to depression. I believe if your life is full of having positive (aka-happy) thoughts you will be better for them.

This may sound simple, but I think it's a strong-minded person that can control his or her own feelings. Practice at a young age to learn to control your thoughts and feeling. Let them serve you and make you the person you want to be. I am reminded of the Nat "King" Cole song "Smile."

You choose how you feel and what you think. Don't leave it to chance or allow others the authority to control your happiness.

UR *how you make yourself feel!*

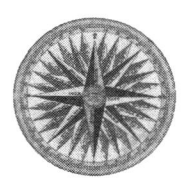

"The road to happiness lies in two simple principles: find what it is that interests you and that you can do well, and when you find it, put your whole soul into it -- every bit of energy and ambition and natural ability you have."
-- John D. Rockefeller III

8 BOUNDARIES & IMPROVEMENT

Stretch your boundaries. Continuously improve yourself. Be comfortable being uncomfortable. Embrace change and think of yourself as adaptable and able to do many different things. Stretch your limits and get out of your comfort zone.

I recall being at work trying to run a report that needed to be presented to the board of directors. I didn't know how to run the report and the person that did was out of town. I needed to add a person to the list. I was so concerned that I couldn't run the report in the format needed, I left out the entire report and told the head of HR that I couldn't provide the list. He reached in his desk drawer and pulled out a pair of scissors and told me, "don't let technology get in the way." I added the name alphabetically and cut and pasted the name in the report. This might sound ridiculous, but it really changed how I looked at obstacles, boundaries and technology. Use everything to your advantage. Create your own positive momentum and don't let obstacles stop you.

A dictionary is accurate and very good for what it does, define words. The Internet makes words flexible and dynamic. You can search for words, images, videos, people and businesses related to a topic.

Think of yourself like the Internet versus a dictionary, limitless, without any boundaries. Be flexible, constantly improving, adding new content, and become more meaningful in thought and behavior to evolve into a better person.

UR the person you make yourself into!

"As long as a person doesn't admit he is defeated, he is not defeated...he's just a little behind and isn't through fighting."
-- Darrell Royal, Texas football coach

9 CAREER & SUCCESS

Many people believe you are what you do. It is often the question people ask others to get to know them better, "what do you do for a living?" There are many assumptions made about people because of what they do. I think that's why it's so important to do what fits you and what you fit. Almost anyone can tell you, if you do what you love it's not work.

My advice is simple, do what you love and be the best you possibly can at it. You will be successful and have fulfillment and satisfaction with your career if your heart is in it. However, do not sacrifice your family, relationships, or those you love for your career, losing those people will nullify any career success you may enjoy.

I grew up never knowing exactly what I wanted to do in life. I spent time going through, unsuccessfully, many majors during college. I also had several jobs that I didn't really enjoy. Some people know at age six (6) they want to be a firefighter. They have an unwavering commitment to their calling and pursue it. I think this is wonderful and they should remain committed and dedicated to that pursuit. Others, like me, don't find that passion, rather something they are very good at in a place they fit. When I was young I had an interest in coins and in school I was always very good in math. So it should be no surprise that I ended up doing executive compensation after also getting an MBA. Try lots of things! Broaden your experience base when you are young to learn what drives you and what your passion is.

Success can be defined many ways, but I believe setting high personal standards and achieving those is success. Obviously there are standards to meet in every job, but these can almost always be met simply through hard work. Never let others define your success or happiness. The definition and responsibility for achievement should be self-driven with a strong self-commitment.

UR successful if you are true to who you are and what you enjoy doing.

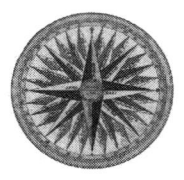

"All I would tell people is to hold onto what was individual about themselves, not to allow their ambition for success to cause them to try to imitate the success of others. You've got to find it on your own terms."
-- Harrison Ford

10 CARING

If you really care about someone you will show it in your words, your treatment of them, the care, time, thoughtfulness you put into the gifts and things you do for them. It can be the simplest of things. For example, when you borrow something return it in better shape than you got it. How you treat the things you borrow is a reflection of how you feel about the person you from whom you borrowed it. How about sending a thank-you note? Or maybe just a quick call or text to say hello to a friend or a new acquaintance.

Remove the phrase, "I don't care" from your vocabulary.

When you walk down the street, do you say hello to people you pass? This demonstrates that you are aware of others and their place in your surroundings.

How about those you love? How do you show them you care? Are you kind to them? Are you considerate of their feelings? Do you put their needs before yours? Don't take advantage of those you love by not demonstrating how much you love them. Share with them how you feel, good and bad. Tell them how much you love them. Don't assume they know, tell them and show them as often as you can. Make it a habit and genuine from your heart. If you care, it will show.

UR *who and what you care about.*

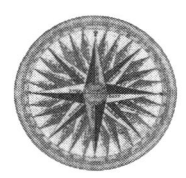

"Look at everything as though you were seeing it either for the first or last time."
-- Betty Smith

11 CHILDREN

No words can describe the feeling of having and raising a child. But the two that most often come to mind are pride and joy, like the song. Pride in everything they do because you feel like you are some small part of it and joy that they are part of your life.

Cherish your time with them; they are your legacy, the part of you that remains long after you leave this world.

Teach them everything you can. Be patient and allow them the time and circumstances to learn. Encourage them to share their thoughts and feelings with you. There is nothing more rewarding than having an open dialogue with your children. Children, share with your parents. Let them help you with their experiences and insight.

I have always said, "I have nothing better to spend my money on than my children." Every dime and every moment of time invested is an investment in your children's future and your own legacy.

My wife and I have put our trust and faith in our children and we have tried to put them first in our lives. Children should recognize the efforts, love and example their parents have set, and cherish your time with them, as I hope I have done with my parents.

UR *the legacy your children provide you.*

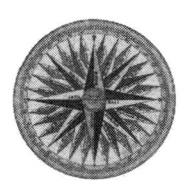

"Making the decision to have a child - it's momentous. It is to decide forever to have your heart go walking around outside your body."
-- Elizabeth Stone

12 CLEANLINESS & APPEARANCE

This may seem like an odd topic versus the other things here, but I think being clean and taking care of yourself and your surroundings says a lot about who you are as a person.

Take personal pride in your appearance, as it is a personal reflection of who you believe yourself to be and of your own self-worth. Appearances, particularly first impressions, can be important and lasting. Imagine you knew that tomorrow you would meet your spouse for the first time. What would you do to prepare, to impress, to make a lasting memory for them?

Cleanliness is the basis for good health and is an important reflection of self-worth as well. Too often we place ourselves second. My wife has been a great teacher for me about this. If you can't take care of yourself, how are you going to take care of others? Taking care of the things under your control, cleanliness of self and environment and your appearance are all things you can control. Many teenagers resist this lesson of cleanliness and use it as a way to differentiate themselves from their parents or show independence and control over something and forgetting the more important aspects of creating good habits and creating a high self-worth.

Like many other things, this is something that is often learned from experience and watching others. Being clean and taking care of ourselves is something all of us can do.

How we feel about ourselves is directly visible in our cleanliness and appearance.

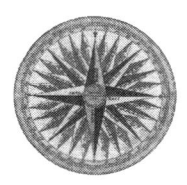

"Be the change that you want to see in the world."
-- Gandhi

13 CHARITY

Giving money and time is a great way to live one's life. I think what you learn through charity is that it truly makes life more fulfilling which is why giving is always better than receiving. Giving to causes or people you care about is even more important. Remember to take care of those closest to you, family, friends and those in your community.

Remember charity starts at home. Give with no expectation of payment in return.

Be generous with your time, they demonstrates that you care which may be the best form of charity.

UR the results of the goodwill and charity you provide.

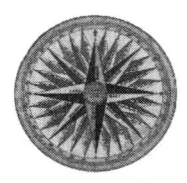

"Blessed are those who can give without remembering and take without forgetting."
-- Elizabeth Bibesco

14 CHOICES

Life is about experiences and choices. Own the choices you make. You can choose to work hard in school. You can choose to have a positive outlook on life. You can choose to drive drunk and kill someone's loved ones in a car accident. These are choices we can make, or not make.

Think about the choices you have made in your life. Are you proud of all of them? Have you made the best choices for you, your family or others? Be responsible for your choices in life and the results of these choices, good or bad.

Remember, it's never too late to choose to do the right thing. It may not generate the outcome you want, but as long as you are breathing you can make choices you believe to be the right ones for you and have a fresh start. Every day is a new day.

Everyday choices determine who you are and who you will ultimately become. Don't underestimate the importance of the little things you do everyday. Focus on these things and make them meaningful for you and others.

For example:
    Choose to be happy today.
    Choose to send a thank-you note to someone today.
    Choose to do what you think the right things are for you
        and your family everyday.

UR the person you choose to be!

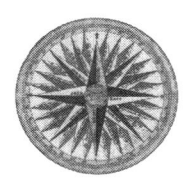

"Destiny is not a matter of chance, it is a matter of choice; it is not a thing to be waited for, it is a thing to be achieved."
-- William Jennings Bryan

15 COMMITMENT

Commitment is like hard work, anybody can give it regardless of brains or brawn. Yet not everyone becomes committed to the things he or she values, believes in or works on. Whether school, work, church, family, community, or country, you should have a commitment level that reflects what is important to you.

Women often talk about men being afraid to commit. If commitment is not given freely, it is not commitment. There are many analogies that come to mind; if you're not with me you're against me..., the train's leaving the station, are you onboard or not? Commitment is the difference between a goal and a wish, and of course, you can't be half pregnant.

Only goals worth achieving or love worth having requires full commitment. What are you committed to? Are you willing to stay the course, never give up and put in the hard work necessary to truly achieve something great and worth having?

UR *what you are committed to!*

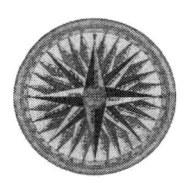

"When nothing seems to help, I go and look at a stonecutter hammering away at his rock perhaps a hundred times without as much as a crack showing in it. Yet at the hundred and first blow it will split in two, and I know it was not that blow that did it, but all that had gone before."
-- Jacob August Riis

16 COMMON SENSE

My parents left me a legacy of common sense. This is one of the most important things they tried to teach me. Common sense means thinking ahead about the next obvious step or conclusion in a scenario. For example, if you punch someone, the obvious and logical conclusion is that you are likely going to get hit back. It's common sense that tells us this.

It's all about forward thinking and thinking through scenarios before you act. It is the basis for many activities, sports, chess, driving and problem solving. It should be a class in grade school. People should take responsibility for taking the information they have and thinking through scenarios and applying common sense. Instead many people are lazy in their thinking and allow emotional responses to substitute for planning and forward thinking. Be responsible for the results of the decisions you make.

Be responsible, train yourself to utilize the information you have, problem solve and anticipate what will happen in situations by using common sense. Think for yourself; don't let others think for you.

UR *the common sense you display.*

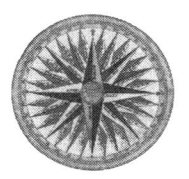

"Common sense is the knack of seeing things as they are, and doing things as they ought to be done."
-- Harriet Beecher Stowe

17 COMMUNICATION

One of the most important things we do in life is to communicate. It is what allows us to love and be loved. It can be verbal and non-verbal, intentional or unintentional or real or misinterpreted.

I remember in college learning that we spend 15% of our life reading, 10% writing, 30% talking and 45% listening. This has always made me think it is extremely important to listen carefully. As I have grown older, my view has evolved in that I believe I must have a viewpoint and be able to converse and interact with someone to be a good listener.

Being a good clear communicator is meaning what you say and saying what you mean in a simple concise manner. Your attitude, eye contact, voice inflection, volume, defensiveness, and facial expression all help to shape how you are viewed by others to be treating them. Communication starts with you! If you are nice, others will be. If you are caring, others will be. If you create a positive interaction with others, you will be viewed positively.

Communication is often like a mirror and people tend to reflect others behavior. The smartest and most strong-willed of us create the environment, drive the conversation, the tone and attitudes we want to have portrayed. The best of us create a positive, energetic, productive and personally fulfilling environment for others. They say character is revealed when no one is watching; I think it is revealed minute-by-minute in your attitude towards others, both people you love and people you don't even know.

People in leadership and authority positions have a greater responsibility to treat others appropriately. Don't get me wrong, there is a time and place for everything including yelling, throwing things and general anger. Not to hurt others, but make the appropriate point. I once worked with someone, a chairman of a company, that would ask me how I was and how my family was doing. He put me as a person before work and took time from his day to do it. More impressively he and his companies significantly outperformed the market. These are the best of people. Anyone can be in charge and be an asshole, that's not impressive. Being the leader and setting the best example is very impressive.

Think about what you do to communicate in a positive, constructive way with others, especially, with the people you love. It is your responsibility to act right. How do you treat them? Show love to the people you love. As the bible says, "Do unto others as you would have them do unto you." (Luke 6:31)

UR *what you communicate.*

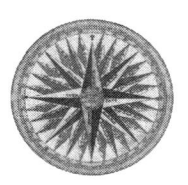

"True eloquence consists in saying all that should be said, and that only."
-- La Rochefoucauld

18 COMMUNICATION (NON-VERBAL)

Be cognizant of non-verbal clues given by others. Often how people behave reveals more about what people think, than their actual words do.

Understanding how you behave and react can send intended and unintended messages to others. This is why telling the truth and meaning what you say is so important. If you are honest, your body language will support it. Various cultures also have many non-verbal cues; understand what they are when visiting other places or trying to assimilate into a school, job or country. Understand how you say something can be as important as what you say.

Train yourself to respond appropriately in words and actions to others. Send the messages you intend to send with a smile, look, nod, posture, position of your feet, shoulders, back, eye contact, eye movement, etc. Be self-aware.

UR *the messages your body language sends.*

"It is good to dream, but it is better to dream and work.
Faith is mighty, but action with faith is mightier."
-- Thomas Robert Gaines

19 CONTROL & RESPONSIBILITY

Own your own actions and their results. It is up to you to be responsible for your own actions and your own life. Take control of your life and don't leave it to fate or happenstance. Be courageous and have convictions about things that are important to you. Own your happiness, your attitude, drive, emotions and how you treat others. To the extent you can control your health and fitness take care of yourself. When you or loved ones have medical problems confront them head on. Many events, important events are not in our control, including sometimes health and disease. Focus on the things you can control (i.e. attitude, happiness, etc.) and focus yourself on the positive; not letting the disease (negative) change who you are, stay in control of your life. Don't let disease of any kind (money, cancer, a bully) control your life.

Don't let others control you with their words, expectations or actions. Make your own choices and live with them and don't look back. In the same vein don't be controlling of others, rather have high expectations that they will make good decisions. Embrace freedom and free will and the idea that everyone is and should be responsible for their own actions, successes and failures. With freedom comes great responsibility for one's own actions.

UR responsible and in control of your own choices.

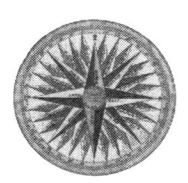

"Find joy in everything you choose to do. Every job, relationship, home...it's your responsibility to love it, or change it."
-- Henry Ward Beecher

20 CREATIVITY

Morpheus from "The Matrix" said, "Free your mind." Structure and organization help us comprehend and understand our surroundings. School, parents and experiences teach us to think and do things a certain way.

Flex your brain. Remove boundaries and problems. Don't spend so much time worried about what the issues might be and focus on what could be. Give yourself thought time, or soak time to consider alternatives and be creative. Creativity takes time, but I also believe it is a practiced skill set. The more you practice the better you become at being and thinking creatively.

Being creative with thoughts and ideas is one of the things I truly enjoy doing. I think a smart and quick sense of humor is part of that skill set too. Everyone can think of the obvious things, value is added when you can view the world from a creative and potentially unique standpoint.

"It's kind of fun to do the impossible."
-- Walt Disney

21 DECISIONS

Take control of your life and the decisions you make. What you decide to do defines who you are. Be mindful of your daily choices and decisions. Think about how you arrive at decisions daily. Do your decisions match your value system and who you want to be? Do you let challenges, obstacles or "perceived challenges" get in your way of your achievements or making the right decisions?

I am very thankful for my college education that my parents provided me. I stayed close to home and commuted to college at California State Polytechnic University at Pomona, aka, Cal Poly. It helped me figure out what I wanted to do for my career. However, I think about how I arrived at the decision to go to school there. I had friends that were going there, it was a good school, close to home and affordable. These are all valid reasons to make the decision to go to Cal Poly.

What I did not do in my decision making process is truly think about the art of the possible. I limited my thinking to what would be easiest for me and my family. I certainly knew there were other schools, but I did not focus on challenging myself or considering that other schools might be even better for me. I applied to just one school.

Don't limit yourself. Don't make challenges (like money), obstacles that you don't even try to overcome. Think hard about the limitless possibilities before you make a final decision. Let your mind create opportunities for you, not limit them. It's all about how you think about the possibilities before you make the decision. Be confident in your decisions and don't spend time looking back. Know that you made the best decision you could based on the information available to you at the time.

"If passion drives, let reason hold the reins."
-- Benjamin Franklin

22 DEMEANOR

I am reminded of the analogy of the duck on the lake. On top the duck looks like it's just floating, underwater he is paddling like crazy. Display a confident and appropriate demeanor in even the most difficult situations. Panicking, complaining, and worrying are never the path to success.

My friend often uses the analogy of the pause button. Before you react, particularly when in writing or on the Internet consider waiting and reflecting on the outcome, reactions or results of what you might write or say.

Right, wrong or otherwise, how you react, your demeanor, demonstrates who you are toward other people. Your character, confidence, values are displayed everyday in how you react. People who are calm and confident are generally thought to be smart. We make judgments, even if very subtle about people all the time. Whether correct or incorrect, your demeanor will influence what others think about you.

Try not to let your emotions run too high or too low in any situation. Be passionate and show your emotions based on your values, and try to remain rational and respectful to others.

Manage your demeanor in all situations.

UR *the demeanor you display.*

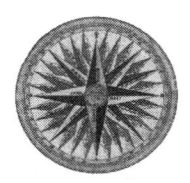

"It is a glorious achievement to master one's own temper."
-- Anonymous

23 DIFFICULTY

Life's not easy, but you probably know that. There will be problems and obstacles in your life. The real question is, how will you react in these situations? Do not blame others or feel self-pity, that leads to unhappiness. Be strong of mind and grounded in your values, problem solve what you can and have a positive attitude as you move forward.

Are you making things more difficult than they need to be? If you change your attitude and outlook will things get better for you and those around you? Make life easy and enjoyable for yourself and those around you. With a good attitude, plan and be thoughtful about others and their time. Be proactive about making things better. Putting others in difficult situations because of lack of planning and thoughtfulness is selfish and inconsiderate.

Remember, if you think things are difficult they will be. Use the tools self-confidence, perseverance, love and a positive attitude to overcome all situations.

UR *responsible for making things better for yourself and others.*

"I love the man that can smile in trouble, that can gather strength from distress, and grow brave by reflection."
-- Thomas Paine

24 DREAM

Be an overachiever. Think BIG, Dream BIGGER!

Think constantly about who you should be, what you should be doing, how you should treat other people, how you should treat yourself and then go out and do it. Let your dreams and imagination expand your capabilities and the person you can become. Use your talent and time to be the best person you can. Do not waste your time on things you don't believe to be important. Set goals and work tirelessly to achieve them. You will achieve more than others and more importantly, more than you ever expected.

Train yourself to dream, be creative in your thinking and limitless in your ideas, love and passion. You are capable of everything you can imagine.

UR *what you dream you can become!*

"You see things; and you say, 'Why?'
But I dream things that never were; and I say, 'Why not?'"
-- George Bernard Shaw

25 EDUCATION & INTELLECTUAL CURIOSITY

Constantly improve your thinking and view of the world. For young people education is everything. Learning how to think is the basis for being able to function as an adult.

Being educated has nothing to do with knowing things; it is about application and analysis. It is taking all the experiences and knowledge you have gathered to assess information and make calculated assumptions and decisions everyday and then building on that the next day.

Make learning and education extremely important in your life, particularly when you are young. As you get older the time you have invested educating yourself should transition into educating others.

Schools are important and should be valued centers of learning by everyone individually and as a society. Teachers are highly undervalued by our society, but also don't underestimate the role of parents in education as well.

Own your own education. Don't blame others for lack of success in this area. There are many forms of education, but don't forget the two most important, experience and failure.

Education can be achieved through hard work and dedication. Both are things you can control. Put in the time and effort to be thoughtful about issues, topics and current events. If you invest the time to research and think, you will be successful over the long run.

Drive your own education by being intellectually curious.

If you don't know something, look it up.

Don't sit idle.

Explore, experience life and try new things. Comfort and lack of challenge are the enemies of thoughtfulness, clarity of thought and being educated. Challenge yourself!

UR a product of your intellectual curiosity and your pursuit of education.

"When I examine myself and my methods of thought, I come to the conclusion that the gift of fantasy has meant more to me than my talent for absorbing positive knowledge."
-- Albert Einstein

26 ENJOYMENT, FUN, LAUGHTER

Spend as much of your life as possible enjoying your work, your play, yourself. It will make you a better person and others around you happier.

It's that simple.

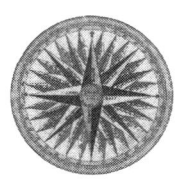

"To laugh often and much; to win the respect of intelligent people and the affection of children...to leave the world a better place...to know even one life has breathed easier because you have lived. This is to have succeeded."
-- Ralph Waldo Emerson

27 ENTITLEMENT

My hope is that we are all entitled to life, liberty and the pursuit of happiness. The way I look at it, the rest of what you get you have to earn! Don't live your life with the notion that you are owed anything.

Work hard to give more than you take and don't give a second thought to what you are entitled to. Expect to work for everything you have.

UR *what you work for.*

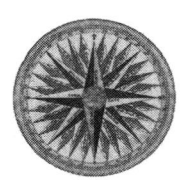

"Reflect upon your present blessings, of which every man has many -not on your past misfortunes, of which all men have some."
-- Charles Dickens

28 ENVIRONMENT

Your surroundings; what is the world that you choose to live in like? You are where you work, live and breathe. Most of us, particularly in the free world get to select what environment we live in. Environment over time creates culture and certain behaviors. Areas like Seattle have increased levels of depression due to the lack of sun. If you live in a beach community you will certainly have a different life and life experiences than if you live in the Swiss Alps. Be aware of your surroundings and the affect it has and will have on your life.

Your environment is not just physical. The people you are surrounded by can also create an environment that is positive or negative, supportive or demanding, cruel or loving. Be a strong person and create the environment you want to live in. Live in your world not the world others want you to live in. Selecting and creating an environment that is enjoyable to you is one of the biggest keys to happiness.

UR *the environment you create and live in.*

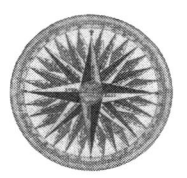

"People are always blaming their circumstances for what they are. I don't believe in circumstances. The people who get on in this world are the people who get up and look for the circumstances they want, and, if they can't find them, make them."
-- George Bernard Shaw

29 ETHNICITY, RACE & FAMILY HERITAGE

Embrace your family history and background; it has helped to shape who you are. Be respectful of others with backgrounds and from cultures different from you.

My father traced my family history to a Cook that came to the United States from Ireland in 1801, subsequently settling in Pennsylvania, then moving to El Paso, Texas. My grandmother's family was from New Mexico. Ultimately, my father moved to Southern California where I was born and raised. My mother's family was from Poland/Russia and my grandmother and grandfather arrived through Ellis Island in the early 1900's. They learned English, but insisted my mother only spoke English. They settled in Dorchester, Massachusetts. They focused on assimilation and making sure their children were American to provide them with better opportunities in life. I think of myself as an American.

My wife, Jacqueline's father was French Canadian and mother's parents came here around 1910's from Sicily, Italy. They all settled in Providence, Rhode Island. My wife has truly embraced her heritage. As an adult she has learned to speak Italian and returned to Sicily and reconnected with her mother's family and her Italian roots. It has been a great life experience, and we have met some great people. So embrace who you are and where your family originates, but embrace the culture of the country you live in as well.

Remember to value the freedom of the individual and not to judge others based on their race, religion, gender or aspects of who they are. Judge individuals based on their intent, behaviors and actions, if you have to judge at all. Be a great representative of your race, culture and country.   Expect the same of all others.

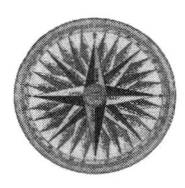

"A man travels the world over in search of what he needs and returns home to find it."
--George Edward Moore

30 EXAMPLES

Whether as a parent, coach, teacher, leader, friend, citizen, worker, teammate, or classmate, what you do provides an example to everyone. Focus on being a good example because you represent yourself, organizations you are associated with, and your family in everything you do.

This is always easiest to see in children mirroring and repeating what their parents do. Also as a leader, you demonstrate values, belief and culture in what you do, say and how you behave. Demonstrate the example you want others to be. If you are a good example, over time you will see others model your example. Don't be a hypocrite...you can't have expectations for others that you don't demonstrate yourself.

When your young watch carefully the examples set by others and choose to model the best of them. As you grow set great examples as you lead and mentor others.

UR *the example you set for others.*

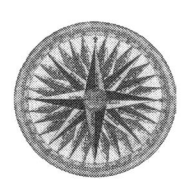

"True religion is the life we lead, not the creed we profess."
-- Louis Nizer

31 EXPECTATIONS

We all have expectations based on our experiences, what we are taught by our parents, friends, family and what we see in the media (i.e. society). We have expectations about how others should act and behave. Some of these things are reasonable, like walking down the street and expecting not to get robbed. Others are not so reasonable, like I don't understand why everyone doesn't think what I think or vote the way I do, etc. These societal expectations are basic and needed for civilization to function. These differences are often the basis for war.

More important to me is how you, as an individual, set expectations. To become a reliable, respected person set expectations for your own behaviors and meet them. These are often simple things, but it's following through on your promises, day after day, that is a great accomplishment. Although, stretching your goals and commitments is often well intended, it can sometimes do more harm than good. A great example of this is being late. If you constantly commit to being on time, but then are late, well intended or not, people won't believe you to be reliable and rightfully so. Simply, give yourself more time, set achievable goals and meet them. Manage others expectations of you. Own your own commitments.

Also important is to manage your expectations of others. Be a strong and supportive influence on others to encourage their achievements and confidence.

As a parent I have extremely high expectation for my children's behavior. Although sometimes not achievable, setting these expectations extremely high as a parent or leader helps a person drive and stretch self-expectations. If done positively, this can be a great source of personal growth. If used as a hammer to show underachievement all the time, this can be a deflating negative and destructive practice. Build your children up with positive expectations that help them to have high expectations for themselves.

UR *the expectations that you meet.*

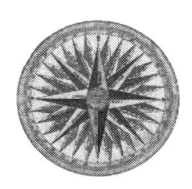

"Keep away from people who try to belittle your ambitions. Small people always do that, but the really great make you feel that you too, can become great."
-- Mark Twain

32 EXPECTATION SETTING

Don't surprise others without a warning. Prepare others for things that may happen in the future. The quickest way to lose trust and creditability with someone is to surprise them with unexpected bad news.

For example, coming home from school with an F on a report card could mean several things to your parents, you had a difficult class, a tough teacher, you didn't try, or you didn't work hard enough. If you didn't set expectations and they are surprised, they will begin to guess at the reason why and will not trust you as much in the future, rightfully so. Rather, if you came home the first week of school and discuss the class your concerns and over the next few months demonstrate responsible work habits and communicate your performance, you will build trust rather than lose it. The F maybe disappointing, but better than losing the trust of those that support you. This same lesson applies at work and in your personal relationships.

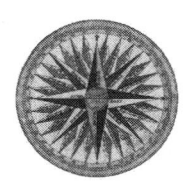

"The shortest and surest way to live with honor in the world is to be in reality what we would appear to be."
-- Socrates

33 EXPERIENCE

Life is all about experiences.

Experience is the best teacher, it's the reason older people are wiser than younger, it can be joyous and torturous and it's the one thing none of us are born with but all of us acquire.

As we go through life choosing our friends, the neighborhood we live in, the food we eat or where we work, we are determining what those experiences will be that shape our lives, our thinking and our legacy. Respect your elders and honor their experience as valuable. Experience comes in two-forms: quality and quantity. Both are equally important, don't undervalue the importance of either. The best analogy I was ever told about experience compares life to a mountain. As you begin life you are at the base of the mountain and your view of the world is simple and self-centered. You are only exposed to things immediately surrounding you giving you a myopic view of the world. As you climb the mountain of life you come to see how the world lives, and your view of the world expands.

We can't control all of our experiences, but think about how your life and view of the world would change with different experiences. Manage and create great experiences in your life.

UR *a reflection of your experiences.*

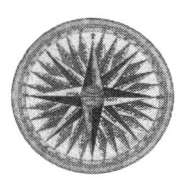

"Judgment comes from experience, and great judgment comes from bad experience."
-- Robert Packwood

34 EXPLORATION & INNOVATION

Humanity has been built on growth and expansion. Exploring the sea, the land, the body and space. The constant pursuit of creative and innovative ideas is at the heart of humanity. It is why we created communities and share our innovations to improve life for everyone.

It is truly amazing the amount of change and innovation over the past 100 years or so including electricity, cars, planes, phones, computers, the Internet, space travel, etc.

My expectation is that change and innovation will continue to accelerate. Embrace change, innovation and exploration in your life. Be aware of the pluses it provides and aware of the unintended consequences it may create. Don't fear it, prepare for it and utilize it to help you.

"All big things in this world are done by people who are naive and have an idea that is obviously impossible."
-- Dr. Frank Richards

35 FAILURE

How do you react to failure? Try harder the next time or quit trying?

Learn from your mistakes and don't repeat them. Failures are as much and sometimes more important in our lives than successes.

I was once told a story about a man that worked for a company and made a million dollar mistake. When the CEO was asked should he be fired, his response was, "no, we just invested a million dollars to train him." This is a very positive way to view failure and often the right one. We all make mistakes; the real question is how do we respond to them. I am sure the worker in the story won't make the mistake again or he should be fired.

UR *the sum of your experiences, successes and failures.*

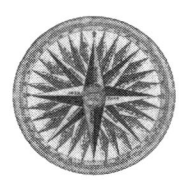

"Forget past mistakes. Forget failures. Forget everything except what you're going to do now and do it."
-- William Durant, founder of General Motors

36 FAMILY

These are the people who know you better than you know yourself. They are people that see you at your best and your worst. They are people you should trust with helping, supporting and guiding you in good times and bad. These are people you should love and support throughout your life. I have always felt that it is my responsibility to help family in whatever they need. I think of my family as an extension of me, so how can you not help yourself? I have been blessed with a wonderful family, I hope that I can and that I do contribute to the success, happiness and integrity of my family and I wish the same for all families!

There are many definitions of family. There are those who are blood relatives, but true family are those you want to share all aspects of your life with. My wife is my closest family member yet we are not blood related. I have never liked the "in-law" description for someone; it almost implies they are only legally part of the family. My wife has always treated my parents like her own, that is family!

When joining a family whether as an infant at birth or as an adult through marriage think of your role and contributions carefully. What defines you more than your family? You are your family.

I tend to think of life in my family in thirds. During the first third (about until age 25 or so), it's your role to fit in. Make things better with your participation. The second third, about age 25 to 50 or so, is when you have your own family. This is your time to influence and significantly contribute to ensuring your family and the broader family are successful together, and on its own. It is up to you to define how broad your family circle is and own successes and failures of that group. I expect that the older you get the larger the circle becomes. If the family is not working well together, it's your job to help make things better. The last third, around age 50, is yours to lead and leave a legacy, essentially yours to run and influence as you see fit, including oversight, stewardship and passing the torch to the next generation. Your role becomes maintaining the family bonds as generations grow up and start their own families.

Each third is training for the next. The example you set will guide future generations on their view of family, their view of their family, what that means, how it works, what their role and responsibilities are and ultimately what type of family and love for each other they will have.

Not everyone has the benefit of a strong family environment. I believe (and hope) that strong families promote values and are the basis for great societies and happiness.

Families should care for each other, even when things are difficult. Everyone should feel a strong obligation to care for those that love you and brought you into the world, regardless of how strained your relationship maybe at times. Love and care for them, particularly when they can't take care of themselves. Everyone needs this type of love and support at some point; fulfill your responsibility to give it.

Children grow up, become adults, learn to be independent and should contribute to the success of the family. Don't tear down the family bonds; the goal should always be to provide more love and caring than you receive. It is your obligation to care for your parents when they can't care for themselves. (Just as they did for you. Even if you think they were not great parents, it's no excuse not to be a great child and person. Always do the right thing.) Children should feel it is their obligation and honor to help their parents and family members when needed. I have certainly felt that way and was very glad to be able to care for and love my parents this way; to the extent they needed it.

Do your part to participate, support and create the family you want to have. It will be the most valuable and rewarding thing you ever do or have.

UR your family.

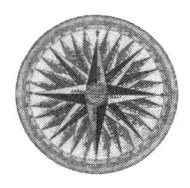

"Too many people overvalue what they are not and undervalue what they are."
-- Malcolm Forbes

37 FIGHTING & SELF-DEFENSE

Don't let yourself be bullied, either mentally or physically. Defend your character, values, wealth, relationships, family and your life. Be strong of mind and character. Do not react emotionally, but thoughtfully and measured.

Make sure you don't present yourself or your family as weak or victims.

Put yourself in situations where you don't need to fight. Fighting, like war, should be a last resort for defense only, but if you are going to fight make sure you win.

UR as tough as you make yourself.

"Tough times never last. Tough people do."
-- Robert Schuller

38 FOCUS

The ability to focus on the task at hand is critical to improving performance. Eliminate distractions and obstacles to success. You have seen basketball players shooting a game winning free throw with 20,000 fans screaming, that is focus. Attention to the task at hand. Attention span and focus are learned skills. Train yourself to focus on the moment and the task at hand. Live in the moment.

Focus on the tasks at hand. Don't let past failures keep you occupied and prevent future success. Don't let the weight of the future and expectations prevent you from doing your best and being focused on what you are doing right now. Use your mind and thoughts to be focused and perform your best.

As Yoda describes Luke's behavior in "The Empire Strikes Back," he says, "never his mind on where he was...what he was doing," counsel that we all need, particularly when we are young. Plan for the future, remember the past, but focus and live in the present.

UR *what you focus on.*

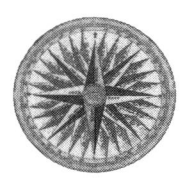

"The height of your accomplishments will equal the depth of your convictions."
-- William F. Scolavino

39 FORGIVENESS

Forgiveness is at the heart of being the good and strong person you should be. Be merciful, forgiving and understanding in every day life. Holding a grudge, being spiteful or revengeful is not helpful. Focus on who you want to be and don't let what others say or do, keep you from thinking and being the person you want to be.

People aren't perfect, they make mistakes. Jesus recognized this while on the cross saying, "Father, forgive them, for they do not know what they are doing." (Luke 23:34) The church teaches reconciliation and it is part of the "Our Father." Forgiveness is a pillar of Christianity. Do not judge others, provide support and forgiveness instead.

Good people make mistakes and sometimes do terrible things. Try to surround yourself with those good people and be forgiving of their mistakes. We have all made mistakes so don't be the first to cast stones at other people, be Christ-like and be supporting and forgiving even when it is difficult.

Choose to be forgiving not vengeful, it will make you a better person.

"The saints are the sinners who keep on going."
-- Robert Louis Stevenson

40 FREEDOM

Freedom is basis for this book and my life. My belief is that I am free to choose, right from wrong, good from bad…I can't begin to understand what my life would be without freedom. I can tell you I am grateful for all the sacrifices made by people and country to allow me this right, and I wish no less for anyone else on this planet in current or future generations.

There are many types of freedoms, freedom of speech, freedom of religion, freedom to pursue happiness, freedom of opportunity. With freedom comes great responsibility to allow others to look, be and act differently without prejudice. It can be a difficult balance as we all often have strong beliefs about right and wrong.

You must allow others to freely have and express their opinions. We all have different opinions about what is best for society as a whole.

Understand when people or groups are trying to persuade or influence you. Use facts to determine what is right. As long as people are free to make choices, society will have to determine right from wrong based on the collective beliefs of individuals. As I have gotten older, I have become more aware of governments, companies and society trying to guide my views of right and wrong and what I should or shouldn't do. Marketing and advertising have been developed for this very purpose, to influence how people think about a product or a topic.

There are many examples of organization or groups trying to influence our thinking. For example, making a lane on the freeway for carpools. This has been proven not to reduce traffic; therefore it is for bad emissions even though the point is to encourage carpooling, which is intended to improve emissions. This is clearly social engineering, in other words the government attempting to change our views and behaviors.

It is fine for these things to be in place, but don't be naive, make sure you are aware of the things, people, companies, and governments in the world trying to influence your views. Make informed conscious decisions about right and wrong.

Be free to make up your own mind about what is right and wrong.

Exercise your critical thinking and freedom of thought.

Be tolerant and respect others freedom of thoughts and actions to the extent that it doesn't hurt others.

You are free. Do not underestimate how valuable freedom is and DON'T LET ANYONE TAKE IT AWAY!

UR free to become the person you choose to be.

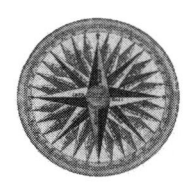

"Posterity! You will never know how much it cost the present generation to preserve your freedom! I hope you will make good use of it!"
-- John Adams, letter to Abigail Adams, April 26, 1777

41 FRIENDSHIP

Very early in life I learned the phrase from a friend: "you are who you associate with." This concept has stuck with me throughout my life. This phrase has many meanings and is the basis for a good friendship. Spend your life with people that build you up and make you a better, stronger, smarter person. Understand the implications of befriending those that don't have your best interests at heart. Do your friends put you first in their lives? It sounds like an easy question to answer, but apply this question to your own life and everyone you have known, did you do this with others?

Your friends are often a great sounding board for what you think is right and wrong. Surround yourself with people of good character and judgment. They are also people who have some great insights in to who you are, often a great source of information for self-reflection. This statement in no way implies that you should only have friends that look, act or have the same money or social status that you do. In fact, variety of thought is the best way for you to learn and test your own values. Testing your values and thinking creates strong convictions, more self-confidence and probably more balanced views.

To have great friends you must be one. As you get older it takes more effort and commitment to your friends to stay in touch and remain close. Make the effort to maintain and build those ties with those most important to you. Remember, it's about quality not quantity. Your number of likes on Facebook is not the same as your good friends. Learn to distinguish between friends and acquaintances.

UR *who you associate with*.

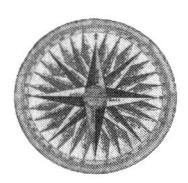

"Shared joy is a double joy; shared sorrow is half sorrow."
-- Swedish proverb

42 GOALS

Ferociously attack your goals; they are the building blocks of achievement, particularly in the stage moving from a teenager into adulthood, when typically one searches for direction, meaning and purpose.

Don't live in fear of what you can't do. Be responsible for the outcomes of your own life. Dream big and then overachieve!

Write down your life aspirations and dreams. Think about what you want your life to have been when you are 100 years old looking back on it. Use your list as goals to achieve. Ask yourself if you are doing the things necessary to achieve the things you want the most. Ready yourself for success. Are you behaving like the person you aspire to be? Own how you feel and how you act. Drive hard in everything you do and you will achieve more than you ever expected.

I have found this type of list to be very focusing, providing perspective and self-motivating. It provides direction when you are searching for purpose in your life. It's also often a reminder of all you have done and all the good things you have in your life, for which you should be grateful.

UR *what you achieve.*

"You can have anything you want - if you want it badly enough. You can be anything you want to be, do anything you set out to accomplish if you hold to that desire with singleness of purpose."
-- Abraham Lincoln

43 GOD

I am Christian, more specifically Catholic. I believe in a higher power and the hope for life beyond what we have here on earth.

I have found Jesus to be the ultimate example of how to live my life, how to treat others and how to lead through service. When you feel you have lost your way in life don't forget to turn to the bible or your local priest for guidance.

My religion has been a blessing in my life and I believe has made me a better person. I have also found prayer and self-reflection to be great tools to make sure I am headed in the right direction in life. Each Sunday I reflect on what I have done right and wrong and feel like I have a clean slate for the week ahead.

I believe in tolerance toward all religions. I also believe we are all honoring the same God. However, I have no tolerance for religions or extremist that call for the death or exile of others. For example, Hitler hunted down the Jews in the 1930's and 1940's. Also, the more recent slaying of Christians in the Middle East and the constant and historic attack on Israel and the Jewish people. The world should not tolerate this type of treatment of others for what they believe.

Remember Jesus said the most important commandments are, Love God with all your heart and soul and love thy neighbor as thy self. This is a great and simple rule to live your life by.

"The various religions are like different roads converging on the same point. What difference does it make if we follow different routes,
provided we arrive at the same destination."
-- Gandhi

44 GOVERNMENT & POLITICS

A friend once told me there is a big difference between a statesman and a politician. I tend to think of politics in a very negative way. The art of manipulating people or things, to get an outcome you want. A statesman has very honorable intentions and does what is right for the greater good. In my lifetime Ronald Reagan has been a great example of a statesman. I would encourage you to study the lives and beliefs of Ronald Reagan and Abraham Lincoln. Both were courageous and not afraid to make unpopular decisions to generate the right results.

I believe in the civil society of the world today, government is necessary. In an ideal world it would not be. In the U.S., our government has been based on the idea that the people have the power and they elect representatives. The more populated our country and the world becomes, the more difficult it becomes to feel "represented." I believe in our system, although far from perfect, is the best example in the world today. Remember, you have to believe in the values your country displays and encourages. Our country should set the moral and ethical standard for the rest of the world. In the U.S., we support the ideals of freedom and the right to life, liberty and the pursuit of happiness. We should display these values in our lives and expect the same from all other U.S. citizens. How can you expect to live in the best country in the world, if you don't make it that way?

UR *the country you represent.*

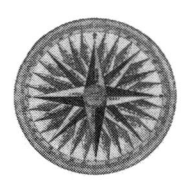

"I desire so to conduct the affairs of this administration that if at the end I have lost every other friend on earth, I shall at least have one friend left, and that friend shall be down inside of me."
-- Abraham Lincoln

45 GRATITUDE

Live your life in gratitude for what you have, what others do for you and for the people you love. It is difficult to be unhappy with your life and your decisions if you are grateful. I think of being grateful as a very positive and unselfish state of mind, where you are acknowledging all that you have and all the people who help and support you.

Gratitude is selfless and demonstrates that you care about others as much or more than yourself. Gratitude can be given for free and will be one of the most meaningful gifts you will give others in your life.

I have been fortunate in my life to have benefited greatly from many people around me including my parents, mentors, friends and family. I have found the best way to repay those who have done so much for me is to be truly grateful for all they have done. The second way is to do for others. I often think about how much my parents provided for me with their limited finances and time. I have always known that I would repay them by doing the best I could to help my children in growing up to be ethical, quality people and good citizens.

Gratitude can be see in how you behave and what you say. Mind your words and actions and make sure they appropriately reflect your gratefulness.

UR truly grateful when you think about others before yourself.

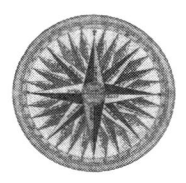

"You have it easily in your power to increase the sum total of this world's happiness now. How? By giving a few words of sincere appreciation to someone who is lonely or discouraged."
-- Dale Carnegie

46 GREED & POWER

You probably know the phrase, absolute power corrupts absolutely. And that nothing good has ever come from greed. I think much of history is written about the quest of both of these human lusts.

I would tell you that true fulfillment comes from being the best person you can be. Being greedy to be the best person you can and powerful over one's own thoughts and actions. Not greed for money and power over others.

I am reminded of the many super heroes in the comics with great powers and the quote from the Spider-Man movie: "With great power, comes great responsibility." Whether the head of a country, a company or your family, act upon the greater good and not self-interests.

Materialism is the enemy of putting others first. Don't let the materials of the world dominate who you are and who you want to be as a person.

Recognize these traits in yourself and others and make sure you don't allow power and greed to affect your lives and actions negatively as they have done so many times to so many people throughout history. Don't let history repeat itself with you.

Don't let power and greed dominate your choices in life.

"True happiness is not attained through self-gratification, but through fidelity to a worthy purpose."
-- Helen Keller

47 HARD WORK, MOTOR, DRIVE

Hard work is the secret to success. To qualify this I would say, working hard on the things most important to you is the secret to life.

Each of us comes into the world the same way and what separates us is what we accomplish while we are here. Focus, determination, high energy, positive attitude and a strong motor are things that we can all bring to our life and those around us everyday. Idle hands are the devil's workshop; not sure if that's true, but it sounds right.

Your actions, both successes and failures are a reflection of what you have spent time on in your life. Obviously, these things are important or you wouldn't spend time on them, right?

Motivate yourself.

Create your own drive and momentum.

Motivation comes from within, but often others can inspire or spark our drive.

I can recall very vividly being in 7th grade at school. My parents had to meet with my teacher. I had a very positive review and I can remember her telling my parents, "he maybe able to go to college and graduate." Although, this was intended as a compliment to me, I remember being upset that the word used was "maybe." In my mind there was no question that I was going to be successful and graduate college. I wish I did not need that spark and could have motivated myself better everyday. However, there have been a few of these kinds of wake up calls for me in my life and I have tried to embrace them and push myself harder.

Look for ways to motivate yourself and constructively challenge others.

Hard work is at the heart of the entrepreneurial spirit.

My wife's career has been a wonderful example of what you can achieve with handwork. I have watched my wife tirelessly dedicate herself to working everyday on her business. She started in 1997 opening Jacqueline's Home Decor on just a credit card. Today she is a respected business woman in Claremont and runs one of the best antique stores in the area. I am very proud of the small part I have had in this, but her daily effort, work ethic and dedication has been the key to her success.

Work tirelessly on bettering your life, relationships, career, marriage, parenting, or whatever those things are that you want to define who you are. Don't ever be out worked, that is the only true failure in life. Leave it all on the proverbial field or court!

UR *what you drive yourself to do.*

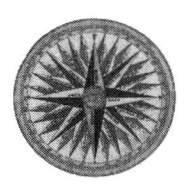

"The person who removes a mountain begins by carrying away small stones."
-- Chinese proverb

48 HEALTH, NUTRITION, FITNESS

This is one of the most undervalued and appreciated elements of life. If you truly love yourself, as you should, health, nutrition and fitness should be an everyday habit.

I grew up with a mother who had health problems from her 30's until age 70. She had kidney disease and was on dialysis for 30 years. She had a positive attitude and never considered herself sick or that there were things she couldn't do. Which is why taking care of your health, mental, physical, dental, nutrition and fitness level is almost inexcusable for the rest of us. My father smoked and eventually got lung and brain cancer. We only get one shot at taking care of our bodies, do the best you can. Eat your vegetables and fruits, brush your teeth at least twice a day, get a dental cleaning every 6 months, exercise everyday, don't over eat, keep stress out of your life, and get an annual physical. These are all easy things to make into good habits.

I think you are what you ingest, whether food, drink, smoke, or alcohol. I believe there is also a mindset that goes with this. If you think about good health, nutrition and fitness you will do the things needed to be healthy. This is one of the best things you can do for yourself. Also, this is one of the best habits you can instill in your children, by example and by force.

UR *what you ingest… food, drink, smoke, alcohol, etc.*

"There is nothing noble in being superior to some other man. The true nobility is in being superior to your previous self."
-- Hindu proverb

49 HOSPITALS & MEDICINE

My father use to say, "more people die in hospitals every year than anywhere else." Kind of a joke, but the concept is right that you should do what you can in life to stay healthy and out of the hospital.

My mother spent much of her adult life in the hospital due to complications from my birth and then subsequent kidney failure. She had a kidney transplant in April of 1980 at St. Vincent Hospital in Los Angeles. The medications used to keep the kidney from rejecting were brutal. She had the transplant for 5 years and survived on dialysis for 30+ years.

Without modern medicine my mother would not have lived to see me as an adult, get married and have a family. I am thankful everyday for all of those experiences. Her attitude was always that there wasn't anything she couldn't do. I never thought of her as sick because she never thought of herself as sick.

Find doctors and hospitals that you trust with your life. Big cities tend to have the best facilities and attract the best doctors. Small towns often don't have specialists and make do with the facilities and doctors they have. This is one of those situations where effort (although nice), is not as important as results. Bedside manner may seem important, but more important is to have an experienced, capable doctor to execute procedures and provide you with the best information to help you and your family problem solve your health issues. This gives you the best chance at successfully beating your health problems.

There were times when we had to be our own doctor. Make hard decisions about what to do or not do. I recall taking my mother out of a hospital hours before they were going to do surgery to improve the blood flow in her legs. It seemed that the doctor was doing the procedure because he knew how, not because she needed it. A second opinion from a surgeon we trusted confirmed that. I was constantly amazed by my mother's resiliency. As a result I have always said, "it is amazing what people can live through." I wouldn't have believed it, if I didn't see my mother do it.

Don't underestimate the importance of the doctor and facilities success rates, go to the best hospital you can find even if you have to travel an inconvenient distance to do it. Lots of people have died from misinformation, surgical mistakes, having unnecessary surgery and just bad decisions. But millions have benefited from modern medicine to live long past expectations. These are risks you have to decide on and often times family members that you trust need to make these important decision for you.

My father died of lung cancer that spread to the brain as a direct result of smoking. He quit almost 20 years before getting cancer. A lesson to young people, don't do things that will shorten your life. There's so much information now about what is good for us; it is easy to make the decision not to smoke, drink excessively or take drugs.

Keep yourself healthy.

Get regular check ups.

Eat right.

Exercise.

Follow grandmother's advice, if you're sick, stay in bed and rest and eat chicken soup. Use modern medicine, doctors, etc, to help you, but know your own body, be your own doctor!

UR *the result of your decisions (and sometimes the quality of your healthcare).*

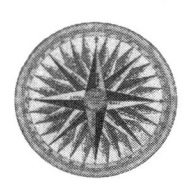

"Life is not holding a good hand; Life is playing a poor hand well."
-- Danish proverb

50 HUMILITY

Don't think you are more important than anyone else. I don't believe in classes, they may exist, but ideally they shouldn't. You're not God, you're no better than the next guy. There are two Bible references I am reminded of. First, the prostitute that was to be stoned. Jesus said, "those of you without sin can cast the first stone." (John 8:1-11) Humble yourself; no one is perfect and neither are you.

Jesus also said, the last shall be first and the first shall be last. (Matthew 20:16) If others are first in your life, humility and selflessness will come easily.

Be humble and self-confident, but don't brag. Let your achievements, character and daily actions speak for themselves.

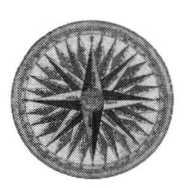

"I wept because I had no shoes, until I saw a man who had no feet."
-- Ancient Persian saying

51 IDK

I don't know. If you work as hard as you can and exhaust all the resources you have it's ok to say you don't know. Not knowing without trying is lazy and a cop out. Laziness is the enemy of being smart, productive and successful.

Many times in life the right answer is not always obvious. Assume you don't know, even if you think you do. Studying, talking and thinking about an issue stimulates creativity and uncovers solutions.

When you're young and lack experience, often you will not know all the answers. When you think you know all the answers you will find that you stop listening to others and getting other view points. Listen to other perspectives before you make up your mind about what is right and wrong.

As you get older you should become more confident about your value system, knowing right from wrong and good from evil. It then becomes your role to identify these things and teach the young people in your life how to "know" the right answers. "Knowing the right answers," means to develop the ability to analyze and think for themselves based on facts and consider others view points.

When I was young, I thought I knew everything. At some point I realized that answers greatly depend on one's perspective. Also, the older I get the more I realize, ...I don't know and that there is no right answer. Knowing you don't know is half the battle, but it should not diminish your effort or intellectual curiosity. Maybe I didn't know everything, but I needed to be able to speak from an educated point of view on topics.

No one knows everything, but how many people are educated and thoughtful about what they say. Have an educated opinion.

UR *what you have learned.*

"A man should never be ashamed to own that he has been in the wrong, which is but saying that he is wiser today than he was yesterday."
-- Alexander Pope

52 INTEGRITY, HONOR, ETHICS

Character is measured by the actions we take when no one is watching. Be of high integrity and character. Mean what you say and say what you mean.

Treat others with respect and dignity. Fight for those who can't fight for themselves. Strive for a world with equal opportunities, not necessarily equal outcomes. Respect others and their right to have thoughts and opinions, even if different from yours.

Honor and respect those who have come before you and those that have sacrificed to give you what you have.

Set extremely high ethical standards for you and those around you and then adhere to them. It really is pretty simple, don't cheat, don't bribe or blackmail others, be honest, take care of borrowed items and leave things better than they were when you arrived. When you borrow someone's car fill it with gas and/or wash it. When you are taking a test, better to fail because you didn't study enough, than pass because you cheated. Tell the truth, lies are the building blocks of deceit, deception and selfishness.

Live and actively demonstrate your values everyday. If you live this way, your values will show up in the things you do everyday. Whether it is helping someone that dropped something, opening a door, thanking a veteran for his or her military service, saying hi to someone passing by or just sending a note to someone.

Build your life around being honest and of high integrity and character.

"Hold yourself responsible for a higher standard than anybody else expects of you. Never excuse yourself. Never pity yourself. Be a hard master to yourself and be lenient to everybody else."
-- Henry Ward Beecher

53 KNOW YOURSELF, THEN IMPROVE YOURSELF

Be self-aware. Understand who you are. Consider the Aesop's fable about the frog and the scorpion.

A scorpion and a frog meet on the bank of a stream and the scorpion asks the frog to carry him across on its back. The frog asks, "How do I know you won't sting me?" The scorpion says, "Because if I do, I will die too." The frog is satisfied, and they set out, but in midstream, the scorpion stings the frog. The frog feels the onset of paralysis and starts to sink, knowing they both will drown, he has just enough time to gasp, "Why?" The scorpion replies: "It's my nature…" Read this story and others at www.aesopfables.com.

The point of the story is that people are who they are. I certainly believe that people will continue to act in a similar manner to what they have done in the past. If someone has consistently lied and not been trustworthy, you should know better to trust that person and you should expect them to act as they had in the past. Don't be the frog.

On the other hand, I challenge you to understand your nature and change and improve yourself, so that you are who you want to be. This is the basis for my book, that you are who you choose to be. Recognize when you are the scorpion or when you are the frog. (We are all scorpions or frogs at some point.) Know yourself, then improve yourself.

UR *who you choose to be!*

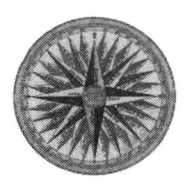

"Never mind what others do; do better than yourself,
beat your own record from day to day, and you are a success."
-- William J. H. Boetcker

54 LAWS & AUTHORITY

In America, we live in a country of laws. The people have willingly given authority to lawmakers, judges and law enforcement through voting and citizenship. No society is perfect and no laws and authorities are perfect. Make sure that what society believes is aligned with your beliefs; if not, vote, write letters and support a peaceful protest. Be the vocal solution and patriot, to shape societies thinking.

Your morals and values should generally align with laws of the country. Laws and authority are necessary tools to help resolve disputes between individuals.

Parents and family are the first line of law and authority. They set the standard and should guide our children to be productive law abiding citizens.

UR the country you live in.

"There is only one success - to be able to spend your life in your own way."
-- Anonymous

55 LEADERSHIP & INSPIRATION

There are millions of pages written about leadership and inspiring people. There are many examples in history. In my lifetime I think of Ronald Reagan, who I felt unified the nation. Magic Johnson who led the Lakers with tremendous work ethic, a positive attitude and great smile, battled HIV and then became a successful business man. He followed his dream. John Wooden who's coaching transcended basketball into life. These are three of my favorites.

I have my own biases, which define great leadership, i.e. strong values, hard work, inspiring others through high integrity, strong beliefs and a constant example. A great leader knows how to delegate by empowering people without the use of fear. As President Reagan said, "trust but verify" individuals with responsibility, not micromanage.

More importantly to me is that you focus on leading and inspiring your own life, career and persona. "Lead" the life you want. If you are passionate about who you are, what you do and what you believe, you will lead and inspire yourself.

UR *the leader of your own life.*

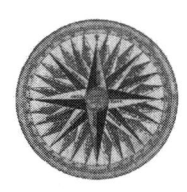

"Do not wait for leaders; do it alone, person to person."
-- Mother Teresa

56 LIVING & DYING

One of my favorite movies, "Shawshank Redemption" said it best: "get busy living or get busy dying." Life is all about experiences and relationships. The more you do and the more you do for others, the better your life is. My mother was ill with kidney failure most of her adult life. She never complained and never let it stop her from living. She continued to be an artist, entrepreneur (selling Tupperware) and being a wonderful mother.

Now as an adult with both of my parents gone it has become more apparent how death is part of life. Without the inevitability of death, life would not be so precious. How they lived their life is a legacy that I continue to learn from and those memories continue to shape who I am.

Do not underestimate the impact your life has on others through the example you set. Life is precious and short, value it and embrace it positively every moment.

Live until you die.

Don't waste a moment!

UR *how you have lived.*

"It ain't over 'til it's over!"
-- Yogi Berra

57 LOVE

One of the greatest human emotions is love. Love is an intense feeling of affection for someone or something.

Both of the greatest commandments contain the word love. Love the Lord your God above all else and love your neighbor as yourself. Simply put love God, others and yourself. Words to live by. If you do this everyday, I guarantee you will be proud of the life you have lived.

Love has to be freely given and is only true love if nothing is expected in return. Love with expectations is not an "intense affection" it's more like a trade or negotiation. How can love be conditional? I would argue it can't be.

You can't make someone love you. That is the toughest thing about love, just because you love someone, doesn't mean they will love you. Everyone knows this, but it still hurts when it doesn't happen. I think when you're young what you also don't understand is that just because someone you love doesn't love you back, it is not the end of the world. The trick is to find someone with whom your love is mutual. The old saying is true, better to have loved and lost, then to never have loved at all.

Take a chance on love, express your feelings. They make you who you are, there's no right and wrong. Not taking a chance to express your feeling is a real opportunity lost.

Don't fear love, it's a good thing, just keep in mind the commitment you are making when you say you love someone. It's a statement about how you feel; no expectations of a reaction should be attached, unconditional.

True love is the ultimate weapon and defense to all that ails you. Replace all your sadness, hurt and anger with happiness, forgiveness and love.

Remember that love conquers all!

Like all other human emotions love can grow or fade. Again, this is a natural thing. Love is a journey of affection. Like taking a long road trip, the speed varies, the road changes, the weather can affect the trip, it depends on the car you're driving, etc. You can't expect the trip to be perfect with no stops, but you can make sure you take the occasional drive down PCH, or the detour to Vegas. The journey makes it interesting and makes the love shared between two people truly their own.

Love intensely with no expectations and be true to yourself.

UR *who and what you love.*

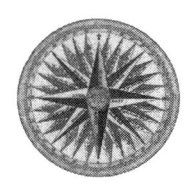

"When you trip over love, it is easy to get up. But when you fall in love, it is impossible to stand again."
-- Albert Einstein

58 LOYALTY

Loyalty is an unwavering personal commitment to someone or something. I have found that in today's world the value of loyalty in society has been diminished and replaced with self-importance.

Maybe it's just nostalgic on my part, but it seems that growing up the concept of loyalty to school, friends, and family was very important. Being loyal means you might be sacrificing opportunities in order to put others first in your life. But it also creates wonderful opportunities, friendships and self-satisfaction.

Like trust and credibility, loyalty not earned, is also not lasting, nor as valued. Derrick Jeter's career was spent with the Yankees; he was also a great player. Part of what makes him a great player is his commitment to the team, the sport and leadership. Without that commitment (loyalty), his influence on the team and organization wouldn't be nearly as impactful.

Use loyalty in your life to demonstrate commitment to your family, friends and organizations important in your life. It is a way to give back for what they have done for you. It costs you nothing, but to give of yourself.

UR *who and what you are loyal to.*

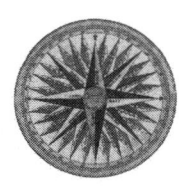

"Individual commitment to a group effort, that is what makes a team work, a company work, a society work, a civilization work."
-- Vince Lombardi, American Football Coach

59 MAKE THE BEST OF SITUATIONS

Life's not perfect. The most successful and I believe happiest of us all make the best of every situation and everyday. We can only control certain aspects of what happens to us in life. We can't always control what is happening to us, but we can control our reactions to situations. Challenge yourself to make good situations out of difficult ones. Challenge yourself to react positively and constructively in difficult situations. Meet difficult challenges and situations head on and turn them into wins.

It's really about being positive and persevering. I am often reminded about making the best of situation at work. Many times we are asked to do things at work that are difficult or beyond our skill set. Dig in focus and produce the best work you ever have. Make this a habit and a way of life.

It's a lot like buying the ugliest, trashed house in the neighborhood and fixing it up. The neighbors are happy it's getting cleaned up and there is a lot of self-fulfillment and satisfaction that comes with a job well done.

Turn the biggest problem or challenge into your greatest success.

UR *the success you create*.

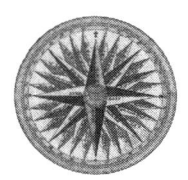

"If your ship doesn't come in, swim out to it!"
-- Jonathan Winters

60 MARRIAGE

Marriage is one of the biggest commitments you can make in your life. (The other equivalent is taking religious vows.) Both require a personal choice to remain faithful and committed for the rest of your life. Marriage is a serious commitment, which requires a conscious decision for a lifetime. I am not sure when you're young if you realize the real commitment. However, it is all dependent on finding the right person to share the rest of your life with.

I have been very lucky to have found my wife Jacqui. I was 21 when we met. We fit very well together. We came from very similar backgrounds, values and religious beliefs. I don't think these are requirements for marriage, but being able to agree on things, like how to raise the kids, what to spend money on or where to go to church, is very helpful. Like every other relationship you must expect there will be sickness and health and good times and bad, the real objective is to support one another through all of these things, otherwise known as love. Even when I am an asshole, I know my wife loves me, even though she may not like what I have said or done. Be understanding and listen intensely for the intent and message being sent by your spouse. Consider how your actions and behaviors send messages to your spouse. Are these the messages you are trying to communicate? Think twice before you say or do something hurtful.

Make sure you and your spouse like, love, trust, have sexual chemistry, compassion and support each other as a couple and as individuals. Put your marriage and your spouse first, even ahead of your children (some of the time). If your marriage is successful and there is love, your children will see this and benefit from it. Don't underestimate the example you set for your children in demonstrating what marriage is and should be.

Communicate, communicate and then communicate again. Share your feelings good and bad. Learn how to share with each other and problem solve together.

I am a firm believer that a spouse should make you a better person. Said better, you should be a better person with them, than without. This falls in the category of; you are who you associate with.

They say love is blind, so listen carefully to those who know you and your prospective spouse well. They know whether you fit well together. Be sure you are making the right decision for yourself and then jump in with both feet and be committed. Remember that you are marrying a person and usually into a family. Embrace and be committed to them as you would your own family, because they are yours now and you are theirs.

UR *who you marry and commit to.*

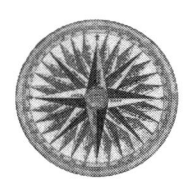

"Grow old with me! The best is yet to be."
-- Robert Browning

61 MEDIA

Media is "a" source of information. Search for the truth, which is a culmination of lots of opinions, including your own. Just because it's in writing doesn't make it true. Always consider the source. Is it a reputable and ethical person presenting the information? Do they have personal views or interests they are trying to promote? Have they made honest errors? Use common sense as your guide and don't over think things.

Media views tend to evolve and change with the views of society. Determine what views are correct for you and don't let society or media norms prevent you from believing in your values. Being politically correct hides and distorts real opinion. Allow others to believe or think what they want, even if you believe them to be wrong. Over time the truth will be revealed. Use facts, experience and history as the basis for your thinking, beliefs and opinions. Try not to let emotions overly influence your beliefs, but don't ignore them. The basis for a free society is that we should be free to do what we want, as long as it doesn't hurt others. Moreover, we should be free to think what we want, freedom is lost without it. Media often tries to shape your beliefs and what you think. Be an independent thinker!

Also, be careful what you place on social media, it can distort others view of you. Perception is often confused with reality.

You have the freedom to think what you want!

UR *what you believe.*

"To avoid criticism, do nothing, say nothing, be nothing."
-- Elbert Hubbard

62 MESSAGES & INTENT

Everything we think, say, and do sends messages to others and ourselves, verbal and nonverbal. Learn to control and manage these messages. Make them positive, constructive and motivating. For example, make sure your spouse knows that you love them through all your thoughts, actions and words. Also, make sure the things you say, think and do allow you to love yourself.

When listening to others look for the intent in what they think, say or do. Culture, tone, mood, lighting, surrounding noises, etc., can all obstruct or misconstrue the messages others send. Everyone makes mistakes or bad decisions, but if the basis for those decisions are ethical and of high integrity, then I believe them to be honorable. Look for the intent in what others say and do.

UR *the messages you send to others and yourself.*

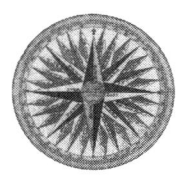

"But try, you urge, the trying shall suffice; The aim, if reached or not, makes great the life: Try to be Shakespeare, leave the rest to fate!"
-- Robert Browning

63 MONEY

Learning how to think about money and how to make money work for you will be one of the most important things you learn. Money isn't everything, but it can allow you to spend time and resources on the things that are most important to you in your life, i.e. visiting family, creating a home for your family, supporting children, buying your wife flowers or a diamond to say you love her. Money is a means to an end; it's not the end.

Most people think you get a job so you can buy what you need and survive. When you don't have any money that is the only choice you have. However, the goal should be to live beneath your means, especially when you are young and invest your money. Money should be thought of as a tool to make more money. The more you save the sooner your job becomes less important to your life and life style.

There are three main components to money, making it, spending it and investing it.

Making Money - A friend once told me make as much money as you can, as fast as you can, and retire as soon as you can. Unless you are independently wealthy there is only one-way to make money, work. Get a job or be an entrepreneur, work hard and save your money. Get your education; it is the basis for many high paying jobs. Work a lot. Be the best at what you do and you will be paid well for it. The best at every trade gets paid well. The best plumber in the world makes quite a bit more than the average college graduate. Do what you are best at; ideally it is something you enjoy. Because we all spend so much of our lives working, don't spend it on work you don't enjoy.

Spending Money - Spend money on things that will benefit you in the long run when you are young. Do not buy things you can't afford. Debt is for suckers. Don't buy things you don't need. Don't buy a $100 pair of pants when you can buy a $30 pair or go without if you don't need them. Spend your money on things that appreciate like stocks or houses. Things that grow in value and will leverage and grow your money. Don't spend money on a new car when you don't own a house.

Investing Money - For me, my house has been my best investment. For example, if you buy a house for let's say $200K and you put $40K down 20%. Then, if the real estate market grows 5% a year you are making 10K per year, which is 25% per year on your original investment of $40K. In other words, leverage your money. The same can be done with stocks. Learn the power of compounding. If you compound your investment every year eventually you will make most of your money from interest and more money than you will ever make from a job if you are patient. My long-term goal has always been to live off of 1/2 of the interest from my investments. Not sure if I'll get there, but I believe it's the right perspective to have about money.

There are many guidelines for money, I believe in the 50-35-15 rule. Live off 50% of what you earn. Invest 35% of what you earn. Give 15% of what you earn to charity. Charity comes in many forms, help others is the basic idea. I will tell you I haven't always been able to follow this, but I believe it is the right goal to have. As you get older it should become easier to achieve this. When you are young, your responsibility is to support yourself and your family. You are your own charity. If you take care of yourself and your family while you're young, you may be in a better position to help others as you get older.

Everyone has to find his or her own way when dealing with money. Be smart not wasteful. There is no magic formula just be disciplined work hard and watch what you spend. Make quality investments and smart decisions with your money and you can have a comfortable life in America.

The goal is to have money work for you!

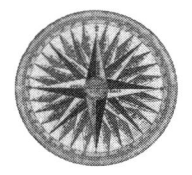

"The real measure of your wealth is how much you'd be worth
if you lost all your money."
-- Anonymous

64 MUSIC, ART, SCIENCE

Be intellectually curious and constantly learn and appreciate how people interact with the world and express themselves. Appreciate what can be learned from others through music and the arts.

I have always found music soothing and comforting in good times and bad. Theater often has provided me with a thought provoking experience, often making me think outside of my box. The visual expression in art has always fascinated me. The stories, history and view of the world through art should be cherished.

Science provides us with an understanding of our world and is also the search for a better future through technology, medicine and many of the other sciences. Embrace knowledge and its pursuit.

Be an appreciator and supporter of the arts and sciences.

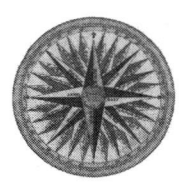

"A musician must make music, an artist must paint, a poet must write, if he is to be ultimately at peace with himself. What a man can be, he must be."
-- Abraham Maslow

65 NATURE VS. NURTURE

I believe we all have free will to make choices and lead our life the way we want. People are certainly limited by their environment, resources, parents or caretakers in making decisions, but strong willed committed individuals overcome these obstacles constantly. Be that person that runs his or her own life and decisions. Don't leave life to chance. Make decisions and own the good ones and bad ones. Destiny and fate are concepts for the weak minded and those that don't want to be responsible for themselves.

We are all products of our environment, upbringing and genes. A big reason I have written this is so that my kids and their kids can learn from my views. Not necessarily agreeing with what I think, but understand that I have arrived at my way of thinking based on influence from my parents, my education, my friends, and my experience. I think that nature and nurturing have worked together to form who I am. I am proud of both of these things and I don't believe they have to be at odds.

UR the result of nature and nurturing.

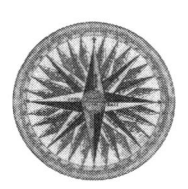

"When I let go of what I am, I become what I might be."
-- Lao Tzu

66 NEGOTIATION, RISK & REWARD

Learn to negotiate to get the things you want. Understand what outcomes are acceptable to you. The old phrase, don't put all your eggs in one basket is a great philosophy to live by. Negotiate from a position of power. For example, look for a job when you have one, you look much more valuable and attractive to the hiring company. Another scenario when you will negotiate is buying a car. Be prepared to walk away if you're not getting the deal you want. Know what the most you will pay is and stick to it. Do not give up your position of power. If you tell the dealer that you need a car to get to work and your car broke down, you have given up negotiating power, and they will know you need a car. Keep information that helps your position.

Most decisions you contemplate in life hinge on understanding risk versus reward. Understand the possible outcomes of your decisions. What is the probability of an acceptable outcome for you? Think about pros and cons of your decisions.

Let's say you buy $1,000 of stock in Disney. What the chances are you lose your investment? How much are you willing to lose? How much do you need to make for it to be a successful investment and in what time frame? Know these things before you act.

Another scenario that comes to mind is negotiating with your spouse. If you win, do you really win? Is it win-win or win-lose? Try to "fight fair" with your spouse without making personal criticisms. Both of you occasionally need to win. I have found having a great relationship is much more important than most arguments, discussions, or conversations that we might have.

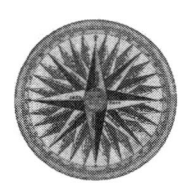

"It is better by noble boldness to run the risk of being subject to half the evils we anticipate than to remain in cowardly listlessness for fear of what might happen."
-- Herodotus

67 OBSERVANT & DETAILED

Listen, learn, observe others and the world around you. Pay attention to details. When you get the details right and understand how things work you will build credibility with others. You will find that sometimes the details are not important to you, but don't forget they may be very personal and important to others. Be observant. Pay attention to details, whether verbal, written or spoken shows that you care about others and your surroundings.

Be smart and use details to your advantage. I remember being at the Chino Airport restaurant with my mother when I was young. We must have sat down five minutes after they stopped serving breakfast, which my mother really wanted. She asked if they would still serve breakfast and the cook said, "no, breakfast was over." Unfazed by his response, my mother proceeded to look over the menu. She found a ham and egg sandwich on the lunch menu. She proceeded to order the sandwich with the eggs on the side over-easy and the bread toasted with the ham on the side. I remember the server being quite upset, but there wasn't much she could do. My mother had breakfast for lunch.

Use details and your observations to your advantage. Watch carefully and learn from everything you see. Surround yourself with smart, ethical people and be observant.

A wise man learns from his mistakes, a wiser man is observant and learns from the wise man's mistakes.

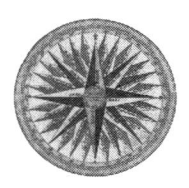

"There was a wise old owl who sat on an oak,
the more he sat the less he spoke,
the less he spoke the more he heard,
we all should be more like that wise old bird."
-- Unknown

68 OPPORTUNITIES

Life is a series of opportunities to do something or not do something. Learning how to decide where to spend your time and money is extremely important.

Think about the spectrum of possibilities and don't limit yourself. Sometimes opportunities present themselves, other opportunities need to be sought out or created.

Where and who will you spend your time with? If you have the opportunity to spend time with bright accomplished people take advantage of it. Should you spend your time at a minimum wage job or spend your time learning a trade, a skill or working toward a degree? You may need to do all of these!

Make smart common sense based decisions with no regrets. Understand the spectrum of choices you have before you make decisions.

Learn to identify opportunities that lead to great things in your life. Meeting your spouse for the first time, meeting someone that might help you someday or the opportunity to help someone else.

Steer away from and avoid opportunities to lie, cheat and steal in any form.

Be an overachiever; do more with what you have than is expected of you. Better yourself. Take advantage of all the opportunities you have. You never know which one will be great unless you try them all.

I think back to obvious opportunities I passed up in my life. I had a chance to volunteer at the 1984 Olympics in LA and didn't. I should have tried to play baseball in high school. I could have applied to more colleges. I can't change these things; I just try to learn from them as new opportunities present themselves. Don't limit what you can do!

It's not just these memorable things, but the opportunities daily to be positive, have a good attitude and help others that are important.

The opportunities you embrace create the experiences that shape your life.

UR the opportunities you take advantage of.

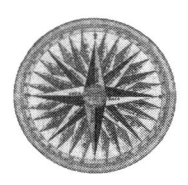

"The greatest achievement of the human spirit is to live up to one's opportunities, and to make the most of one's resources."
-- Vauvenargues

69 OTHERS FIRST

The greatest thing you can do with your life is putting others first. Be giving of your time, be caring and serve others without expecting anything in return. These are the most unselfish and fulfilling acts you can do. I think of all the soldiers, police officers and fire fighters who dedicate their lives and even give their lives in the service of others. There is no greater gift one can give than their life for another person.

Don't overlook the importance of daily good deeds for others. The habit of putting others first daily is just as powerful as giving one's life for another. It can be flowers for someone you love or food for someone you don't know. Be self-confident in knowing you are living life the right way, in the service of others.

I basically believe that people are good. I think believing the opposite is not a good way to go through life. Obviously there are exceptions and to be blindly trusting is naive or even potentially dangerous.

How will you gain the trust of others, if you don't believe in them? Believe in people and you will be amazed at the results.

The saying it is better to give, than receive is true. Try as often as you can to be a giver.

UR *the best person you can be when you're helping others.*

"Thoughtfulness for others, generosity, modesty and self-respect are the qualities which make a real gentleman or lady."
-- Thomas H. Huxley

70 PARENTS

I feel fortunate to have had parents that loved and wanted the best for me, as I do for my children. Remember, parents aren't perfect and are just people. Take the best qualities of each of your parents and use and apply them in your life. Take the worst and don't repeat it! I believe the role of parent is the most important function of society and probably in your own life as well.

I feel bad for all those that don't have parents or have bad examples for parents. Do the best you can in life to help those without this guidance. When they succeed in spite of their parents, we all should be proud of them.

There is more than just a biological reason to have two parents. When kids are young, mothers are the best parents, nurturing, understanding and attentive to the details of taking care of one's self. As kids get older and begin to become independent the father tends to be better at disconnecting and supporting the transition to adulthood. This might be an overgeneralization, but this is how things work. It is great that as parents, we can provide a balanced view of the world for our children. As a parent, try to provide what your children need, not what they want.

The most important thing you can teach your children is to think for themselves. Not what to think, but how to put positive, constructive thoughts in their heads. This will give them a great foundation and kaleidoscope through which to view the world over the rest of their lives. I am reminded of the film "Life is Beautiful." In the midst of World War II, a father shapes how is son views day-to-day life.

Arm your children with the mental fortitude to deal constructively and positively with all the world can throw at them. Teach your children how to react, cope and preserve through tough times.

The other important reason for having two parents is that the battle for power needs to be two parents against one child. The parents should win arguments. It's not a democracy; it's a household that children should be appreciative to be a part of. It is your responsibility as a child, to respect, honor and treat your parents as wiser, more experienced and with the assumption that their views and knowledge have withstood the test of time.

There is no magic to being a good parent, be genuine, be the best example you can and love unconditionally…and do the same for your parents.

"The mediocre teacher tells. The good teacher explains.
The superior teacher demonstrates. The great teacher inspires."
-- William Arthur Ward

71 PAST, PRESENT, FUTURE

Prepare for the future. Sacrifice and hard work early in your life will make for a better future. Look forward in life. I have found that always looking toward vacations, parties, or milestones has kept me focused and hopeful for a great future. I am reminded of it in one of my favorite movies the "Shawshank Redemption"... "Hope is a good thing, maybe the best of things..."

Be mindful and knowledgeable about the past, however, remember you can't relive it.

Be respectful of those who came before you. There is a lot to learn from history, be a student of the past. Understand why things happened the way they did. Remember those who don't know the past are destined to repeat it. The past is the reason I have written this book. As I have gone through life, I have found that I have had the same problems, thoughts, concerns, experiences that so many others have experienced, particularly my parents. I wanted my past experience to provide some insight for others, particularly younger members of my family.

Most importantly, live in the present. Focus on where you are, what you are doing, and how you are acting. Focus on who you are, who you strive to be. Do the best you possibly can at everything you do! Make each moment count. Life goes quickly, enjoy and cherish each moment.

"Finish each day and be done with it. You have done what you could. Some blunders and absurdities no doubt crept in; forget them as soon as you can. Tomorrow is a new day; begin it well and serenely and with too high a spirit to be cumbered with your old nonsense."
-- Ralph Waldo Emerson

72 PATIENCE & WAITING

Patience is a virtue. Being patient is a sign of humility. It demonstrates that you value others and that you don't place yourself above others.

On the other hand, impatience creates a drive and momentum that has gotten great work done. Great inventors don't rest and wait, they push forward.

Both of these thoughts are true and accurate. You must balance these concepts in your life. Impatience at the expense of others is not a good thing. And waiting for something to happen may mean failure in what you are doing, so don't let that happen.

Be thoughtful and measured when appropriate. Be bold and move quickly when needed.

"The strongest of all warriors are these two: Time and Patience."
-- Leo Nikolaevich Tolstoy

73 PATRIOTISM

Patriotism is the act of being loyal to one's country. I am a believer in the basic values and beliefs set forth in the constitution. I am also in awe of the sacrifices made by our military to provide us with these freedoms. The veterans, fallen soldiers, POW's and wounded warriors deserve our countries full respect and honor for their commitment and sacrifice. Regardless if you agree with the policies of the day, the reasons behind the military actions or what is politically correct, these individuals should be honored by our society.

One of my childhood friends, Dion Stephenson, was killed in Kuwait during Desert Storm. We lived down the street from each other for a couple of years in grade school. He was the guy you knew would do well in life. He was always positive, athletic and fun to be around. We did not stay in touch when he moved, but when I heard he was killed in the war; I could not help but think we just lost one of the best of us. He sacrificed everything, to provide the freedom we enjoy. When I see military personnel, I thank them for their service and think of Dion's sacrifice. He defines patriotism for me.

My wife's father (Robert Denis) served in World War II under General Patton in the Army infantry. He stepped on a land mine and was temporarily blinded and injured. He came back from war and worked as a painter for 40 years creating a good life for himself and family. I hope that my generation and future generations understand and appreciate the toughness and sacrifices of the many generations before us. Not all of us are called to be in the military, but our view of these individuals and how we treat them is very important as a society.

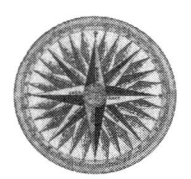

"Few will have the greatness to bend history itself, but each one of us can work to change a small portion of events, and in the total of all those acts will be written the history of this generation."
-- Robert F. Kennedy

74 PERFECTION

It is honorable and appropriate in your life to strive for perfection in everything you do. I believe it is what separates great from good. Have high expectations of others, but higher for yourself.

I am reminded of one of my favorite John Wooden quotes, "perfect practice makes perfect." Do things the right way all the time. Don't be sloppy, even when no one is watching. Good habits are important, don't practice mistakes.

With that said, life's not perfect, others aren't perfect, you're not perfect and your life's not perfect. Embrace this as fact. Do the best you can and be content and happy with the results. Be happy with your imperfect results, if you truly did your best. Don't allow others to define your happiness based on their expectations. This is why you should have high standards, because you are defining success for yourself and owning your results. Don't disappoint yourself; always do the best you can.

Don't allow striving for perfection and not making it, keep you from being happy or being self-content. It is great to be driven, just be happy at the same time.

"The gem cannot be polished without friction, nor man perfected without trials."
-- Chinese proverb

75 PERSEVERANCE & PERSISTENCE

There are several historic and monumental examples of perseverance and persistence including the Great Wall and the Pyramids. Both of these came with great human dedication, sacrifice, leadership and even death. But my basic belief is that over time good, ethical and high integrity values wins out over evil. This may be naive on my part, but it is this basic belief that gives me the drive to be persistent and persevere at school, work, relationships, etc. Without this positive belief that things will workout for the best, I think it would be infinitely more difficult to overcome obstacles and be persistent. My belief that outcomes will generally be appropriate for the amount of commitment and effort I provide and that I have done my best to make things right, is what keeps me focused and driven to see things through.

Focus on the tasks at hand and not the emotions of the situation. Drive to the decisions and outcomes you want to happen and believe to be right regardless of how difficult that may be. Consider the input of others before making these decisions so that you are making informed decisions.

Don't forget there are lots of ways to get to the same destination. Be creative and adventurous; understand that there are lots of ways to do something, not just your way. In fact, others may have a better way to do something, allow yourself to learn the best way. Don't be stubborn by always having to do something yourself or your way.

Like hard work, like attitude, persistence and perseverance can be given for free and reveals one's true character.

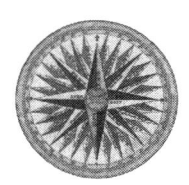

"Don't bother about genius. Don't worry about being clever.
Trust to hard work, perseverance and determination."
-- Sir Frederick Treves

76 PERSPECTIVE

It is important to have a well thought out perspective (and opinion) on topics or situations in the world, and more importantly in your life. It demonstrates that you are thoughtful, but that is just step one. You also need to understand your own values and beliefs and that life is gray, not black and white. Just because you have an opinion doesn't mean it's right. You must test your perspectives against what others think, particularly those you trust and those with experiences different from your own. Experiences create different perspectives and broaden your view of the world and potentially changing your own thinking.

Imagine you are standing in a lush, fruitful valley. You have a certain perspective about where you are, what's around you, what your world is like. Now climb to the top of the mountain. When you reach to top you can see the valley you were standing in, but you can also see other mountains the ocean, the beach and other valleys. You have a whole different view of what the world is like.

Age and experience are like climbing the mountain. This is why you respect your elders and honor their opinions and perspectives. They have seen more than you have.

Keeping your perspective also means making sure you keep your priorities straight. Make sure the things most important in your life are treated as such.

Is God important in your life?

Is family important?

Are you important?

Do your actions reflect these beliefs?

Do not elevate things or people to levels of importance in your life they don't deserve.

Keep your perspective on the things you value the most and make them most important in your life.

UR *what you cherish and make important in your life.*

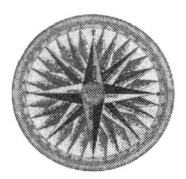

"Maturity is achieved when a person postpones immediate pleasures for long-term values."
-- Joshua L. Liebman

77 PREPARATION

As John Wooden said, "Failing to prepare is preparing to fail." I have always thought preparation is just about putting in hard work and time, anyone can do it. If I really care about something like a test, I would really study hard ahead of time. It's easy to practice things you love to do. Much more difficult for you to engage and work hard on things that you don't have as much interest in. Take personal pride to be prepared, on time and knowledgeable about what you are doing.

What do you really care about? Family, friends, community, marriage, work, fitness...? Do you spend time and effort to make these things what they should be? What about you? Are you preparing and doing the things needed to be the person you want to be? Are you working hard enough? Are you making good decisions about where and how you spend your time? Are you getting an education or learning what you should do to be successful? Are you practicing the skills you need to be successful? Are you listening and learning from the right people?

Abraham Lincoln said, "Give me six hours to chop down a tree and I will spend the first four sharpening the axe." Prepare yourself for success and to have the life you want, do the right things, work hard, and be the person you strive to be starting this moment. Each moment counts. Prepare by training your mind to be in control of the thoughts that go through your head. Like a boxer training for a fight, ready your mind for the challenges life throws at you. The better you prepare your thinking and behaviors for the things you want in life, the better chance you have of achieving them.

UR *who you have prepared to be.*

"What ought one to say then as each hardship comes?
I was practicing for this, I was training for this."
-- Epictitus

78 PRIDE

It is important to believe in yourself and take pride in the things that make you who you are. Make sure that how you feel about yourself and others is reflected in all your actions, not just your words. How you dress is an outward reflection of how much you care about yourself. How do you complete your work, is it detailed, is it thoughtfully done, did you do more than what is expected? You and others should and will judge the type of person you are by the quality of all of these actions. Even when no one is watching, pride is about how you feel about yourself.

Make the world a better place for having you in it!

Be proud of who you are and what you do. If you are not proud of who you are and what you do, you need to change who you are and what you do, right now, it's that simple.

Life isn't fair or exactly the way we want it, but we need to own and be responsible for our place in it. Do the best with what you have and you can be proud of who you are and what you have done.

UR *how you feel about yourself.*

"Character may be manifested in the great moments, but it is made in the small ones."
-- Phillips Brooks

79 PRIORITIES

What is most important to you? Who is most important to you? What do you enjoy?

Spend time on things and with people that make you a better person. Strive to put others you care about first in your life.

In college, I completed a few exercises to focus me on what I wanted out of life. I would suggest you consider doing the same. Here is the note I sent to my son and niece (Heaven) several years ago about priorities and goal setting asking them to think about their futures. See the note below.

"It is important that as you enter adulthood, that you take responsibility for your actions, thoughts, behaviors and the life you lead. How do you make sure you are the person you want to be, the person you should be?

I want to challenge you this summer to spend some time thinking about what is important to you in your life, what things you want to accomplish, what are you driven by, what do you enjoy doing, what do you excel at, and what you want the world (and those you love) to think about and remember you for. How you treat others, who you spend time with, your relationships and how you spend time is very important in determining who you are. You need to live these things everyday, every minute possible. While knowing what you want is important there is tremendous power in writing down these things as it creates commitment and makes you focus on achieving goals.

I don't have to read what you have written, but I would like you to seal it in an envelope for you to read later. It can be as long or short as you want. Think about the ideal you, what things you would do if there were not limits or problems or obstacles in the world, as you write it. Set goals and desires that are real and full of meaning to you.

Here are the 4 things I want you to do.

<u>*First,*</u>
Think about the person you are, your strengths and weaknesses, likes and dislikes. There are lots of free personality tests online.
Take others if you'd like, IQ test, EQ tests...
Write down your scores_____

I am also a big fan of the Meyers Briggs theory of psychological types.

Extraverted (E) vs. Introverted (I)
Sensing (S) vs. Intuition (N)
Thinking (T) vs. Feeling (F)
Judging (J) vs. Perceiving (P)

Knowing yourself and what makes you happy will help you think about how you treat others in your relationships and help you understand what type of career/job might make you happiest. Personality, IQ and who you are does change over time, and you are in control of who you become, it's not set in stone.

<u>*Second,*</u>
Dream about what things you could do and who you might become if there were no limitations in your life and the world. Write down a list of 50 things you want to do in your life. (Bucket List)

<u>*Third,*</u>
Write down the things you want to accomplish/goals in the following areas in your life over the next 5, 10, and 20 years. Some of these might be a repeat from your bucket list, that's ok.

-Self
-Spiritual
-Education
-Career
-Physical
-Health
-Family
-Relationships

-Financial
-Business
-Community/Volunteering
-Country/Citizenship
-Causes you want to support
-Any other areas you feel are appropriate

Also, think about what you need to do to accomplish these things, focus and hard work.

<u>*Last*</u>, *write your obituary. Look at the obituaries of famous people or others online. How do you want the world to remember you? One paragraph only.*

Remember, you control your life, your accomplishments, your dreams and who you are, be strong and don't let the world dictate your life. Sometimes good and bad things happen in life and you have to stay the course and continue to be the person you strive to be. Patience and perspective in life are very important.

You have until the end of summer to complete this.

You are who you determine yourself to be."

My hope is that they would do these things to really, concretely consider what they want and focus them on who they want to be. It is much different to just think of these things rather than actually putting it in writing. I can also tell you that looking back at my own list from 20 years ago is quite insightful. This is why I suggest you dream big. I wish I did not limit my thinking and dreams when I was younger. The sooner you learn to focus on achieving your true dreams and ignore the obstacles the more creative, driven, positive and successful person you will become. This was my hope for them and my hope for anyone reading this.

It's never too late to do your own list.

UR *who you determine yourself to be.*

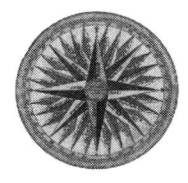

"Find a purpose in life so big it will challenge every capacity to be at your best."
-- David O. McKay

80 PROBLEM SOLVING

Learn to quickly assess problems and move to solutions. If you are very good at this you should not spend a lot of time doing this and you can focus on more constructive parts of life.

When you don't know what to do, get advice from someone you trust. Get help. Don't be too proud to ask for help. Often times you can get to a better answer quicker when you ask others who have experienced the same problems. When you are older, seek out opportunities to help others with your expertise or assistance. Allow others to succeed with your guidance; and provide it as needed. Do not be overbearing, or take over.

Train yourself to think clearly, quickly determine possible solutions and make decisive decisions with the input of others. If done correctly, when you problem solve maintain these four key principles.

1. Focus on the situation, issue or behavior, not the person.
2. Maintain self-confidence and self-esteem.
3. Maintain constructive relationships.
4. Take initiative to make things better.

If you do these things in solving problems and maintaining relationships you may not always be successful, but you can be confident you have done your best and you can live with the outcome. With family, and particularly your spouse, learning how to constructively and jointly solve problems is extremely important to the success of the relationship.

UR *the solutions you create.*

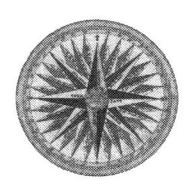

"A great pleasure in life is doing what people say you cannot do."
-- Walter Bagehot

81 QUOTES

I have been a big fan of quotations from various experienced and bright historical figures. I have complied a list of quotes over the past 25 years and occasionally read it to ground my thinking. It reminds me there are some basic truths about how to live one's life that are tried and true throughout history. I have referenced many of the quotes from my list throughout the footnotes in the book.

Two of my favorites are Andy Rooney's "I Have Learned" and the various quotes by John Wooden. Also, consider reading John Wooden's "Pyramid of Success."

"I've learned.... That the best classroom in the world is at the feet of an elderly person.
I've learned.... That when you're in love, it shows.
I've learned.... That just one person saying to me, 'You've made my day!' makes my day.
I've learned.... That having a child fall asleep in your arms is one of the most peaceful feelings in the world.
I've learned.... That being kind is more important than being right.
I've learned.... That you should never say no to a gift from a child.
I've learned.... That I can always pray for someone when I don't have the strength to help him in some other way.
I've learned.... That no matter how serious your life requires you to be, everyone needs a friend to act goofy with.
I've learned.... That sometimes all a person needs is a hand to hold and a heart to understand.
I've learned.... That simple walks with my father around the block on summer nights when I was a child did wonders for me as an adult.
I've learned.... That life is like a roll of toilet paper. The closer it gets to the end, the faster it goes.
I've learned.... That we should be glad God doesn't give us everything we ask for.
I've learned.... That money doesn't buy class.
I've learned.... That it's those small daily happenings that make life so spectacular.
I've learned.... That under everyone's hard shell is someone who wants to be appreciated and loved.
I've learned.... That the Lord didn't do it all in one day. What makes me think I can?
I've learned.... That to ignore the facts does not change the facts.
I've learned.... That when you plan to get even with someone, you are only letting that person continue to hurt you.
I've learned.... That love, not time, heals all wounds.
I've learned.... That the easiest way for me to grow as a person is to surround myself with people smarter than I am.
I've learned.... That everyone you meet deserves to be greeted with a smile.
I've learned.... That there's nothing sweeter than sleeping with your babies and feeling their breath on your cheeks.
I've learned.... That no one is perfect until you fall in love with them.
I've learned.... That life is tough, but I'm tougher.
I've learned.... That opportunities are never lost; someone will take the one's you miss.

UR: You Are Who You Choose To Be

I've learned.... That when you harbor bitterness, happiness will dock elsewhere.
I've learned.... That I wish I could have told my Dad that I love him one more time before he passed away.
I've learned.... That one should keep his words both soft and tender, because tomorrow he may have to eat them.
I've learned.... That a smile is an inexpensive way to improve your looks.
I've learned.... That I can't choose how I feel, but I can choose what I do about it.
I've learned.... That when your newly born grandchild holds your little finger in his little fist, that you're hooked for life.
I've learned.... That everyone wants to live on top of the mountain, but all the happiness and growth occurs while you're climbing it.
I've learned ... That it is best to give advice in only two circumstances; when it is requested and when it is a life threatening situation.
I've learned.... That the less time I have to work with, the more things I get done."
-- Andy Rooney

"Be quick, but don't hurry."
"Failing to prepare is preparing to fail."
"Don't mistake activity for achievement."
"Goodness Gracious, sakes alive!"
"Intensity makes you stronger. Emotionalism makes you weaker."
"If you don't have time to do it right, when will you have time to do it over?"
"Be more concerned with your character than your reputation, because your character is what you really are, while your reputation is merely what others think you are."
"It is amazing how much can be accomplished if no one cares who gets the credit."
"Tell the truth. That way you don't have to remember a story."
"You cannot live a perfect day without doing something for someone who will never be able to repay you."
"Listen if you want to be heard."
"It's the little details that are vital. Little things make big things happen."
"The true test of a man's character is what he does when no one is watching."
"Make every day your masterpiece."
-- John Wooden

"We become what we think about."
--Earl Nightingale

82 RELATIONSHIPS

I was raised in a small family by a mother who had serious health problems my whole life. I learned at a young age to cherish my time with others, regardless of how short or long it is, make sure it is quality time, for it is these relationships that you will remember throughout your lifetime and will eventually outlive you and become your legacy. Your impact on others, and the moral support, love and friendships are what truly make life worth living and are the reason to maximize every valuable minute we have.

Try to be loving and supportive in all your relationships all the time. This should be easy to do with your friends and family. As James Taylor said, "shower the people you love with love," from the song "Shower the People." This is more difficult with people who are not as well meaning to you, but how you behave towards these people is a true depiction of your character and heart. Be grateful to all of those people that think enough of you to spend their precious time on this planet with you.

Be conscious of what kind of relationships you have. What do you want out of these relationships (are you getting it), are they making you a better person, and are they getting something beneficial out of the relationship? What are you doing for them? Don't let bad people or bad relationships dominate your life. Improve your good relationships and get rid of your bad ones. Ultimately how you interact and connect with others is a big contributing factor to who you really are as a person.

UR *the relationships you create.*

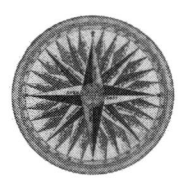

"One of the best ways to persuade others is with your ears - by listening to them."
-- Dean Rusk

83 REST, SLEEP, VACATION

It is important to rejuvenate and recharge your proverbial battery occasionally. If you work hard, you should give yourself permission to rest and relax. I have found that vacations provide time to consider and reassess how you are spending time and whether what you are doing, is what you want to be doing. It also provides time and space to reconnect and strengthen your bond with your family and making memories that last a lifetime.

To make thoughtful well-planned decisions, you need to be rested. We spend at least 25% of our lives sleeping, it is a necessity for the body and the mind. Don't let it dominate your life. Don't be lazy, but be rested and prepared so you can be your best self.

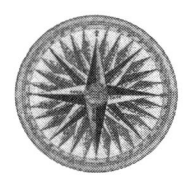

"Always laugh when you can. It is cheap medicine."
-- Lord Byron

84 SECRET TO LIFE

The secret to life is to work hard for all the people you love and things you enjoy, while keeping a positive outlook on the world and displaying a sense of gratitude for all that you have. Secondly, surround yourself with quality, high integrity people, you are who you associate with.

(Watch the movies "It's a Wonderful Life" and "A Beautiful Life.")

UR *the secret to creating a wonderful life.*

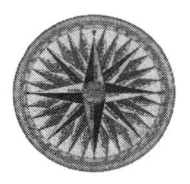

"I'm a great believer in luck, and I find the harder I work the more I have of it."
-- Thomas Jefferson

85 SECOND WIND (NOT QUITTING)

It's not how many times you're knocked down, but how many times you get back up. It maybe cliché and an old proverb, but it's true. Everyone struggles growing up with mistakes, failures, and feelings of underachieving.

Find your drive and motor to pick yourself up and don't quit when things get difficult. Billy Joel's song "You're Only Human" was a great inspiration to me. There are many lessons to be learned in music. When things get tough, I find my resolve in remembering I am not perfect, but what I can do is pick myself back up and try again.

This applies to everything in life big and small. Study the most successful people in history like Abraham Lincoln and Thomas Edison. They failed much more than they succeeded in life. Their continued efforts after failing led them to their successes, their second wind.

I am reminded of this everyday by my son Grant. He has worked hard his whole life. He doesn't know how to quit. He is like the stonecutter that took 101 strikes of the hammer on the stone to break it. It's not that the 100 hits were failures, but the preparation required to make the 101st strike successful.

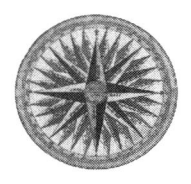

"The three great essentials to achieving anything worthwhile are; first, hard work, second, stick-to-it-iveness, and third, common sense."
-- Thomas Edison

86 SELF-CONFIDENCE

Confidence is a fascinating concept and one you need to personally master. It can be quite a balancing act though. Too much and you are an arrogant ass who only cares about his or herself. Not enough and it is tough to attract others and become great at anything.

The best example is in athletics. A majority of the best athletes that perform well under pressure believe they are the best and that belief drives high performance and success. If they don't believe they can succeed, then why should their teammates, coaches, or fans. These same people do not lose confidence when they fail, otherwise their career is over.

We are not all professional athletes and our own personal disposition has a lot to do with our confidence. I have found that as I have gotten older and care less what others think, and it has been easier to be confident.

This is one of the things parents should encourage in children. Without confidence we would not have made it to America, landed on the moon or built the first computer. Teaching children to believe in themselves will be the cornerstone for future innovations; curing cancer, making the next great screen play or writing a #1 hit song.

I believe we are what we think about. If our mind is full of self-doubt, and there is no room for confidence, then how can we be successful? Fill your mind and the minds of your friends and family with confident successful thoughts and I believe you have a much better chance at achieving the things you want in life.

UR *as confident as you believe you are.*

"Faith that the thing can be done is essential to any great achievement."
-- Thomas N. Carruther

87 SELF-SATISFACTION

If you are not satisfied with the decisions you make and the person you have become, how can you expect anyone else to be? If you are not satisfied, you need to change what you do, maybe who you are. Seek the advice of others close to you, i.e. parents, grandparents, other elders with experience and perspective. The ability to be happy requires that you believe in yourself and know that you have worked as hard as possible to be the best person you can. I also believe to meet your potential in life you need to be satisfied with the result of who you have become as a person. Not selfish, not cocky or arrogant, but confident that with the appropriate effort you will do well, in whatever you're trying to accomplish. Some of us are born extremely confident in oneself. Others need to boost their self-esteem. Know yourself, and move toward the center of the spectrum.

Don't spend your life comparing yourself to others. Strive to meet your self-expectations and be satisfied with the results. You might think this is contradictory to what the best performers do, but I would say it's not. Achievers want to be the best and won't settle until they are. I admire this drive and motor to perform. However, I believe exceeding one's expectations is a greater achievement than meeting that of others. We should know ourselves better than anyone and know what our capabilities are. Michael Jordan had tremendous personal drive, it is what he was known for. He never seemed to be satisfied, he always wanted to be better. This drive made him the best and now that he is done playing basketball he can look back and be self-satisfied that he gave everything he had.

UR satisfied with who you are, if you've done your best.

"What can be added to the happiness of a man who is in health,
out of debt, and has a clear conscience?"
-- Adam Smith

88 SEX & SEXUALITY

Everyone has a different view about sex and sexuality, it its very unique and very personal. Like many of the items discussed here I can only give my opinion.

People are sexual beings. It is the reason we are still on the planet. Be comfortable, not embarrassed about your sexuality. When we are young, we are very curious about our sexuality. As I have gotten older, I think of it as a special bond between husband and wife, which helps to keep that passion and intimacy in marriage. I am and always have been extremely attracted to my wife. This is one of many things that attracted me to her and keeps us happy together.

Be responsible for your sexual exploits. Having sex freely with many partners carries the risks of STD's and pregnancy. Be smart in making decisions about who you choose to have a sexual relationship with. When you are not selective about sex, it loses its meaning and its importance to the one you truly love. Think about what it says about you as a person. What does it mean you think about yourself and others? You wouldn't buy one engagement ring and give it to 10 different girls. You would buy one ring for the woman you love and want to marry. I think of sex, ideally, the same way. With that said, I also believe you need to make sure you and your spouse are compatible sexually. It is an important part of a lasting marriage and it should not be undervalued.

"Happiness is like a cat. If you try to coax it or call it, it will avoid you. It will never come. But if you pay no attention to it and go about your business, you'll find it rubbing up against your legs and jumping into your lap."
-- William Bennett

89 SIBLINGS

I have not had the experience of having siblings. In a perfect world they should be your best friends growing up and a life long confidant and trusted advisor. I believe if others are first in your lives it can work this way. However, the relationships of my friends and family rarely seem to work that well. Like any other relationship, it takes two willing and consenting people to make it work.

I have tried to encourage and I would say even demand, that my kids get along with each other. My hope is that they remain thoughtful and considerate of each other and their families. This is the basis for a strong family. This is what makes families great versus destroying them and growing apart. As they say, blood is thicker than water, and I would add that bloodstains left by sibling rivalry are very difficult to remove.

So often kids are competing for attention from their parents or others. Trying to stand out and be unique as individuals. This is not necessarily a bad thing, but they also need to learn to put others first! If siblings are unselfish I think their relationships can be lifelong and constructive.

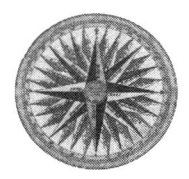

"We can often do more for other men by trying to correct our own faults than by trying to correct theirs."
-- Francois Fenelon

90 SOCIAL ISSUES

There are several social issues which dominate our world right now. I don't pretend to have an answer for these issues, but I encourage you to protect yourself and family, to the extent these things may impact your lives. Also, carefully consider your view of these topics or other world and social events that you think are important. Consider all perspectives and have informed, fact and morally-based views of your own. Remember the more personal these things are the more emotions play a part in how you feel. Here are my simple thoughts:

Family - The importance of raising children and creating family values has been highly undervalued by our society. In my estimation this is a cause of many of the troubles in our current society. Family should come before self.

Euthanasia - Killing anyone, even if for mercy is a slippery slope. Having the government making decisions about whether it is legal to live or die is even scarier.

Mental illness - The identification and treatment of mental illness without social stigma is one of the greatest opportunities we have.

Over population - Many of the global environmental issues we have been caused by the sheer size of the population with no end to the growth insight. I don't have a solution, but I believe it will be the root many of the problems of the 22nd Century, if not sooner.

Drugs - Eradication of drug addition would be as productive as the elimination of cancer. I would argue drugs and alcohol abuse are the cancer of families, societies and countries.

War/Terrorism - There has been war as long as there have been people. It is a difficult decision to go to war and should not be done lightly. War should be used only at last resort to protect ourselves from death and destruction. Terrorist should be considered enemies in a war. These are bad people, committing violent acts against innocent people, there is no religious or other justification for this behavior. The world (countries, governments, religions, organizations and individuals) should all be dedicated to stop this type of behavior.

Abortion - I just don't understand why this is ok? The goal of the world, ideally, should be to never have an abortion. This has nothing to do with a woman's choice for me. This is the legalized killing of millions of people a year worldwide. I understand that there are medical situations where it may be necessary. Or even in the event of rape, I can understand not wanting to raise the child, but maybe the real solution should be adoption, not killing. Think of others first, protect those that can't protect themselves. What kind of society allows someone to say, I don't want someone, let's kill them?

Oppression due to Race, Gender, Religion, Sexuality, etc. - I believe we as a country have come a long way in the last 150 years to overcome many of these issues, but both in the U.S. and the world still have a long way to go. We should not be blind to the refugees, human trafficking and oppression of people across the globe. It is a moral dilemma we all need to acknowledge and not tolerate; it demands a global solution. I hope and believe the ability for people of various backgrounds to coexist will continue to improve with new generations.

Freedom of speech and thought - I believe this is the most important of rights and should be protected above all else. People don't have to agree on everything, but they should be allowed to disagree without being demonized or persecuted by others or the media.

Just some of my thoughts and opinions.

"The higher type of man clings to virtue, the lower type of man clings to material comfort. The higher type of man cherishes justice, the lower type of man cherishes the hope of favors to be received."
-- Confucius

91 SPOUSE

The word itself refers to one of a pair, two people living a shared life. To be a good spouse and to have a good spouse you must first have love for one another. I try to put my wife first in everything I do, although I am not always successful, I do try and have the best of intentions. Communicate and share your feelings so that you both clearly understand, trust and believe one another.

I have been married for twenty-one years. I have been very lucky to have found my wife. We grew up about a mile from each other. We went to the same church, same grammar school and high school and were even born in the same hospital, but didn't meet until college. For this reason we have had many similar experiences and have similar values and beliefs. I believe this has made it much easier for us to be on the same page when making family decisions and raising the children.

I think the key to being a successful spouse is to fully support (I didn't say agree) and enjoy your spouse in all that you do. Enjoy who they are, not who you wish they were. Your presence should make the other person better, more complete and happier over their lifetime. Don't measure success day-to-day or month-to-month, have a long-term perspective. All relationships have ups and downs, remember that together you control your relationship, family and love and happiness. Do not settle for an average relationship with your spouse, have high expectations of them and give them all you have.

UR one of a pair with your spouse.

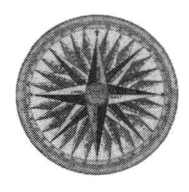

"Courage is what it takes to stand up and speak; courage is also what it takes to sit down and listen."
-- Sir Winston Churchill

92 STRONG OF MIND & COURAGEOUS

Do not live in fear. If you treat others right and you are a good person, be confident in that knowledge. Be courageous living your life. Stand up for what you believe is right. Be the person you know you should be.

I can't over emphasize how important training yourself to be strong-willed and convicted about your values is.

Be in control of the thoughts and decisions you make.

Making decisions because it is easy or safe is many times a good bet. But not making a decision because of the fear of failure (or even the fear of success) is wrong. Make bold decisions in your life. Have the confidence and strength to live out your big dreams. You only have one life to live, make it the best you can.

Be your own best coach and cheerleader. Think thoughts that lead you to success, not failure. (Don't even think the words, "I can't.") Make yourself strong and courageous, don't rely on others to do it. Ask yourself constantly if your thoughts and behaviors make you a strong and courageous person? Do they?

Don't run your life based on fear!

UR courageous!

UR strong of mind!

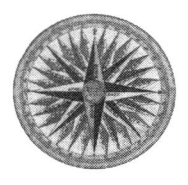

"He who reigns within himself and rules his passions, desires, and fears is more than a king."
-- John Milton

93 TAXES

Jesus said it best, "So give back to Caesar what is Caesar's, and to God what is God's." (Matthew 22:21) Even 2,000 years ago taxes plagued society. I am sure some people think of it as a good thing. I think a small amount of taxes are good. However, a significant taxation can create a powerful government and self-important politicians and redistribute money from those that have made it, to people that may or may not really need it or deserve it. People should be "free" to keep and spend the money they earn. Obviously, a certain amount is required to keep the government infrastructure and military in place. And of course we should help those that can't help themselves.

I can't understand why the government would ever need more than 15% of income regardless of how much you make. If they need more than that, they aren't spending it wisely. I think having an effective income tax of 50%, sales tax, property tax and an estate tax is Un-American. How can you call it a free capitalistic society if we are taxing our population that way? This kind of socialistic view is not what made our country great. How much is too much to be passed on to the government? The reward for the hard work, effort and results should be more than 50%.

My advice is to pay the taxes required, but use the taxes laws in your favor to keep as much of your hard earned money for you and your family as you can. Better for you to direct your wealth to people, charities and causes you believe than allowing the government do it.

It's not always how much you make, but how much you keep.

"What a man is contributes much more to his happiness than what he has, or how he is regarded by others."
-- Arthur Schopenhauer

94 TEACH YOUR CHILDREN

1.) Focus on what is important, prioritize, put things in perspective
2.) Don't be selfish, it ultimately leads to unhappiness
3.) Maintain your personal integrity and character
4.) Accept the things that are your responsibility and act upon them
5.) Accept your failures and disappointments in life, learn from them, don't dwell on them, and teach others not to repeat them
6.) Respect the world and the people around you
7.) Create meaningful relationships based on trust, respect and kindness
8.) You are who you associate with
9.) The secret to success in life is hard work and the service of others
10.) Know yourself and do things everyday that make you happy
11.) Be self-confident and satisfied with who you are
12.) Do something good for someone everyday
13.) Leave things better than you found them
14.) Be a gracious winner and loser
15.) Have situational awareness
16.) Do the best you can at everything you do
17.) Be resilient
18.) Use common sense
19.) Love yourself and allow yourself to be loved
20.) Understand and be able to identify what you want in a soul mate
21.) Take religion seriously - love God and your neighbor
22.) Stop worrying about fame and fortune
23.) Get thick skin. Sticks and stones may break your bones, but names will never hurt you
24.) Don't kill another man's dreams
25.) Perception is half the battle competence is the other half
26.) Acknowledge others' strengths and be tolerant of their weaknesses
27.) No one's perfect, but that's no excuse to not always do your best
28.) Be forgiving and merciful toward others
29.) Be positive, happy and have a great attitude
30.) Follow the Ten Commandments

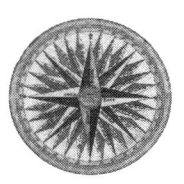

"It is the nature of man to rise to greatness if greatness is expected of him."
-- John Steinbeck

95 TIME MANAGEMENT

No one has enough time. But everyone makes time to spend on things that are truly important to them. You can always tell what someone thinks about himself or herself and others based on how they spend their time. Those that open doors, pick up something that falls or that give without thought of something in return are honorable, thoughtful and selfless, or at least are trying to be. Those that do not make the time for these simple acts are sending the world the message that they are more important than others. They would rather focus on themselves than being concerned or courteous to others. Be giving of your time in service of others, be a selfless person and send the right messages to the world you live in.

You can't save time, you can only spend it, so spend it wisely.

Prioritize the things and people that are most important to you and make time for them. There are hundreds of books on time management. Ultimately, what they tell you to do is prioritize and spend time on the things you want to. Don't let others dictate how, where and when you spend your time. Be responsible for your time and how you spend it.

Life is short, so don't waste time.

Do the things you love and aspire to do.

UR *what you spend time on.*

"To love what you do and feel that it matters -- how could anything be more fun?"
-- Katherine Graham

96 THINGS OUT OF YOUR CONTROL

I am not sure if it is in our nature or something we learn, but what a waste of time thinking about negative things or things not in our control. Train your mind to focus on the positive and things you can control or influence. Trying to control things that we can't is futile. Prioritize things you can do to positively impact yourself and others that you care about.

Do at least one good deed for somebody everyday. Buy someone lunch, say hello to someone you don't know, open the door for someone, be overly nice or friendly to someone. Do simple easy things everyday that you can control and that make you a better person and help those around you. Make it a habit to positively control or influence those things you can, and don't waste your life thinking about things that have happened or things that are out of your control.

You will find it amazing how impactful small simple gestures can be to build relationships and love. A thank you note, a positive supportive comment (rather than being negative), or just actively listening to someone are the building blocks to a life well-lived.

Don't worry, complain, or waste your valuable time on things out of your control. Take ownership and responsibility for your life and all that you can control starting with your own thoughts and actions.

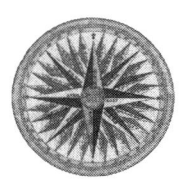

"The person who says it cannot be done should not interrupt the person doing it."
-- Chinese proverb

97 THINGS YOU TRULY OWN

Property, clothing, house, money, cars...you can lose or have any of these things taken from you.

Experiences, love, relationships, family, memories, thoughts...these are things you can keep and truly own.

Foster the growth and development of all of these things, but most importantly those things you truly own. Rich or poor, in sickness or health, you can focus your life on loving others, creating great relationships and having positive constructive thoughts.

Value the right things in your life and appreciate the journey in life building, relationships and love.

UR *the experiences, love and relationships you create.*

"We come into this world crying while all around us are smiling. May we so live that we go out of this world smiling while everybody around us is weeping."
-- Persian proverb

98 THINKING - READING, WRITING, TALKING & LISTENING

With technology the usage of various communications and our skill sets will need to evolve. We will write more and maybe read less than our parents did. Historically, it has been thought that we spend approximately 15% of our life reading, 10% writing, 30% talking and 45% listening. These statistics were highlighted to me in a college communications class. They underscore the importance of listening and made me question how intensely I listen to others. It is important to do all these things well if you want to understand and be understood.

What I have learned since college is that you spend 100% of your life thinking, so I suggest you get really good at that. Think before you act. Learn to be an outstanding problem solver. Create solutions instead of identifying problems. Be smart. If you practice being smart everyday, you will be. Make good decisions about your life. Like Aretha Franklin said, "Think."

UR what you write.
UR what you say.
UR what you THINK!

Thinking is very underrated. You will think during your life at least as much as you will breathe. Even more specifically, we become who and what we think about. Our futures and lives are defined by what we do, but all that we have done has been preceded by what our thoughts have been.

STOP! Think about the thoughts that have gone through your head in the past hour, day or week. If your thoughts were food would you be eating at McDonald's or at a nice restaurant? What's better for your mind, healthy, fresh quality food or McDonald's?

I contend if you have positive thoughts about your family, friends, work, studies, God, your life, yourself, that it will result in positive actions, fulfillment and future in these areas. I think if your thoughts were all driven by the statement below you would live a fulfilled, well-intended life (not perfect, no such thing).

<u>The secret to life is to work hard for all the people you love and things you enjoy, while keeping a positive outlook on the world and having a sense of gratitude for all that you have.</u>

How clearly you communicate with others is a huge part of how you build relationships. Reading, writing, talking and listening skills are critical. Learn and teach your children to be effective and detailed in their communication and their understanding of others. Mean what you say and say what you mean.

UR *what you think about, so think great thoughts.*

"In matters of style, swim with the current; in matters of principle, stand like a rock."
-- Thomas Jefferson

99 TIMING

The phrase we all know is… "timing is everything," but why is that so important? Understanding timing means you understand your environment and your place in it. When dealing with others you need to understand their current situation. For example, walking into your boss' office to ask for a raise when the company is not doing well or laying off other employees is clearly bad timing and lacks common sense.

I am often reminded of a story someone once told me about asking for a promotion. He said it is like buying a train ticket and then waiting for the train to arrive. There is often preparation that needs to be done or experience required before timing is right for a promotion, graduation, change in job, buying a house, a decision to propose marriage and many of our life decisions. Do the hard work needed ahead of time to be ready and prepared for that next step. Once you are ready, be patient. You have purchased the proverbial train ticket with your hard work, just wait for the train to arrive.

If there is an opportunity available consider all your alternatives and make a confident decision. Conversely, if the timing is not right patiently wait and be prepared when it becomes available. Don't let fear of making a bad decision overrule your good judgment.

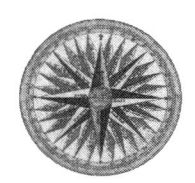

"Genius is eternal patience."
-- Michelangelo

100 TRAGEDY

I have personally been very fortunate not to have had any major tragedy in my life. There are two types of tragedies, preventable and non-preventable. Try to do the simple things in life to prevent tragedies for you and others. For example, don't drink and drive, try not to be in dangerous places, don't be out driving at 2 and 3 in the morning after the bars empty out.

Unfortunately, there are accidents, war, terrorism, etc. that can't be prevented, at least by you. They say time heals all wounds. I think time just puts distance from events. I have also heard love, not time heals all wounds. Allow others to help you get through these difficult times. Use your love and the love from others to heal. Remain active in thought and body. Be grateful for the past and be hopeful for the future.

Find others, that you trust, who have been though similar situations. Share your pain and thoughts. Learn how others cope, survive and effectively move on with their lives.

I know this is a very idealist view, everyone will deal with these events differently, but it is important to revert to becoming a rational, stable and positive person so that you can take ownership of your life back.

UR resilient; teach your children to be as well.

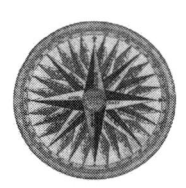

"Man has never made any material as resilient as the human spirit."
-- Bern Williams

101 TRUST

Trust should be earned not given. Of course there are various levels of trust. I trust they will pick up the trash on Thursday. I also trust that the pilot is not drinking and will make good decisions when I fly. As Ronald Reagan said, "trust but verify." My favorite President, and I agree with this statement in many situations, particularly when managing people and projects.

However, true trust comes with no verification, no safety nets. "In God we Trust..." There's no "except when," after this statement. Trust in your spouse, family and good friends should be absolute. Of course if they prove untrustworthy in their words or actions, they have not earned your trust. That's on them, not you. It can be very painful to trust someone and then be disappointed, particularly those close to you. Remember to be forgiving and merciful to those who truly love you.

Be cognizant of how you treat others and who you trust. Do you have an appropriate screen before you fully trust someone? Have the people you trusted truly earned it? Surround yourself with trustworthy people.

UR *who you trust.*

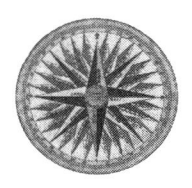

"Aerodynamically a bumblebee shouldn't be able to fly,
but the bumblebee doesn't know that so it goes on flying anyway."
-- Mary Kay Ash

102 UNLEARN BAD THOUGHTS & HABITS

When we are young, we sometimes learn bad habits or learn to view the world and others from a negative viewpoint. Nobody's perfect, everyone can and should improve. Identify these times and events by testing your view of the world versus others who are wiser and more experienced than you. If you are honest with yourself over your lifetime, you will be able to look back and know that you're thinking about yourself, others and the world you live in has evolved. Your challenge is to shape your thinking in a way you can be personally proud of.

I believe as children we can develop these bad habits as a result of our limited view of the world, bullies, difficult environments, lack of love, poor role models, weak family values or low self-esteem. Find great people to learn from and draw from personal strength to continuously improve yourself, your habits and your view of the world.

Unlearn your bad thoughts and habits to become a better you every day. Shape and become the person you dream yourself to be.

UR *the thoughts you have and the habits you display.*

"At first dreams seem impossible, then improbable, then inevitable."
-- Christopher Reeve

103 VALUES

The set of beliefs that govern your life and your behaviors are your values. Everyone is different and therefore have different beliefs and values. Fight hard in your life to stay true to your beliefs and stick firm to those things that are most important to you. Create behaviors and actions everyday that demonstrate your values.

For example, if you value your family demonstrate your love by, doing things for them (taking out the trash), treating them nicely (no bad or defensive attitude), and maybe the occasional gift (flowers, etc). Treat yourself in a similar manner.

Write a list of the things you truly value and believe in. This will create buy in for you and commitment to live your life with these things in mind.

Here is my list:

God/Church - living Christ like

My wife - support, love, honor

My children - guide, inspire, set an example for them

Family - treat them as an extension of myself

Friends - be supportive

Other people - be respectful

Life - respect others right to life and their pursuit of happiness

Freedom - allow others the freedom to do as they wish, as long as it doesn't hurt others

Hard work - effort is the outward display of caring and personal pride

Responsibility - a person is responsible for his or her actions and the result of those actions

Parenting - parents are responsible for caring, teaching, supporting, financing and educating their children

Self-ownership - understand who you are, be proud and confident in that knowledge; be aware of your short-comings and own your failures while you constantly strive to do better

I am sure the list can go on. The one other, sometimes difficult part of values, is to respect the values of others, especially if different from your own. There are as many sets of values as there are people, many of them culturally based as are some of mine above. It's these differences that create political parties, countries and war. But it's also these differences that create different cultures, languages, lifestyles and many of the varieties in life that we cherish. And you know the old saying that variety is the spice of life.

I would expect your personal values to be more conservative than those set by society. If society's broad standards seem difficult to conform with consider re-evaluating your personal values. Always set your value system to the highest of standards.

UR the values you believe in and display.

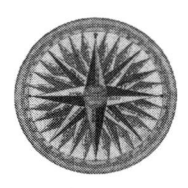

"Beauty, truth, friendship, love, creation - these are the great values of life. We can't prove them, or explain them, yet they are the most stable things in our lives."
-- Jesse Herman Holmes

104 WANTING, WISHING, REGRET

Wanting and wishing are hopeful thoughts about the future. Be careful that wanting and wishing are not in excess and drive bad behaviors and excessive obsession. Money can be a great example of this. Listen to the song by the O'Jays, "Money."

On the other hand, great passion and drive have created some of histories great inventions, stories, films, music, art, athletes and companies. Be passionate and hopeful in your wanting and wishing, but keep perspective about what's important in life.

Don't forget, regret is a backwards-looking exercise. Learn from your mistakes, but don't regret your decisions. Don't beat yourself up for doing the best that you can. No regrets!

UR *what you want and wish for.*

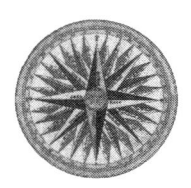

"The past cannot be changed. The future is still in your power."
-- Hugh White

105 WORRY

What good ever came from worrying? Stop worrying, it's a waste of time. Prepare for challenges, embrace hard work and be responsible for the outcome.

Worrying never made anyone happy or successful.

"It doesn't matter how often you get knocked down; what matters is how often you get back up."
-- Vince Lombardi

FINAL THOUGHTS

As I reflect, I tend to circle back to these several concepts that are most important to me.

1. Challenge yourself. Challenge your thoughts and behaviors. Be flexible, creative and open to everything versus stubborn and close-minded.

2. Change yourself. Be a better you tomorrow than you were yesterday. Give yourself time to grow, heal and improve. Stop worrying about whether others can or will change, fix yourself.

3. Be grateful. Selfishness leads to unhappiness. It is very difficult to be grateful and unhappy at the same time. The ultimate goal is to enjoy life and be happy.

4. Serve others. Life is best when you are focused on serving others. Live by the motto, it's better to give than receive.

5. Own your life. Be responsible for who you are, what you do and who you become. Train your mind, which is the most powerful asset you have, to be positive, set aggressive goals/personal standards, and to think things that make you the person you choose to be.

If you read no other chapters of the book, consider reflecting on 79 PRIORITIES, 84 SECRET TO LIFE and 94 TEACH YOUR CHILDREN. These are my favorites.

Carefully consider the choices you make because it shapes who you become and defines your values and your ethics. This book has been a great way for me to reflect on my life, my relationships and my loves. I hope that you can use UR in the way that I have to remind me of the person I have been, but much more importantly, who I strive to be everyday.

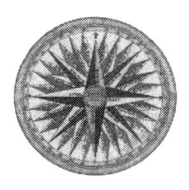

"Remember, UR who you choose to be."
-- Rob Cook

ABOUT THE AUTHOR

Rob Cook is a Human Resource Executive with over 20 years of experience working with a variety of Fortune 500 Companies. He has served in diversified roles that include advising and leading talent development, performance management and total rewards functions in the high tech, engineering, construction, restaurant and retail industries. In 2012 he began R.C. Consulting Services and servers as an Independent Consultant. He advises select high tech companies in areas such as Executive Compensation, Board Pay, Equity Program Design, HR Strategy, Retention and Incentive Plan Design, Proxy Disclosure, Governance Practices, Benefit and Retirement Plan Design, as well as Development and Succession Planning.

Mr. Cook also has been a silent owner in his wife's business Jacqueline's Home Decor. The antique home decor store was started in 1997 and is a prominent part of the Claremont Community.

Mr. Cook has an M.B.A and B.S. from California State Polytechnic University at Pomona. He is happily married to Jacqueline Cook. They live in Southern California and have two adult children, Chelsea and Grant.

Made in the USA
Lexington, KY
12 November 2019